TRICKS to
FREAK OUT
YOUR FRIENDS

Hat out of rabbit!

Blood + guts

Pete Firman grew up in Middlesbrough where his parents and sister provided him with a normal and loving family environment. He studied for an acting degree and looked forward to joining the family business selling secondhand cars, but somewhere down the line something went wrong. After spending his teenage years locked away in his bedroom furiously practicing magic with just a poster of Pamela Anderson for company, Pete saw an ad that summoned magicians from near and far to audition for a new TV program. Clearly, he did what any reasonable man would do in such a situation – he stripped to his underpants in a snowy back garden and filmed himself performing tricks.

The show was *Monkey Magic,* and Pete's career as a TV magician (and as an amateur wildlife cameraman) began. Since then he has performed his own brand of anarchic trickery on Sky One's *The Secret World of Magic*, and amazed viewers and celebrity guests alike with his ability to perform disgusting, painful, and frankly dangerous tricks with animals, cigarettes, and big spiky things on Channel Four's *Dirty Tricks*.

Pete no longer owns a poster of Pamela Anderson; instead, he lives in north London with his girlfriend, a bowl of frightened goldfish, and an ever-expanding magic library (that's a library of books about magic, not one that disappears occasionally). *Tricks to Freak Out Your Friends* is his first book.

PETE FIRMAN

TRICKS TO FREAK OUT YOUR FRIENDS

CHICAGO
REVIEW
PRESS

www.petefirman.co.uk

Cover design: Sarah Olson and Angie Allison
Interior design: Angie Allison
Photographs: Armand Attard

First published in Great Britain in 2006 by
Michael O'Mara Books Limited
9 Lion Yard
Tremadoc Road
London SW4 7NQ
First U.S. edition published in 2007 by
Chicago Review Press, Incorporated
814 North Franklin Street
Chicago, IL 60610
ISBN-10: 1-55652-695-4
ISBN-13: 978-1-55652-695-4
Printed and bound in Singapore by Tien Wah Press Pte. Ltd.
5 4 3 2 1

For Dad, Mum, and Lucy.

Thank you for supporting me every step of the way and never telling me to get a proper job.

I love you.

ACKNOWLEDGMENTS

I feel writing a list of acknowledgments is a terrible mistake as I'm bound to upset whomever I leave out. However, I would like to thank a handful of people.

Derren Brown for writing such a lovely foreword.

Mac King for being so generous with his magic and allowing me to share his brilliant tricks. Check out www.mackingshow.com.

Michael Vine and Heather Holden-Brown for their support and encouragement, and for believing in me and this book.

All my close friends, you know who you are. Without you I wouldn't know what I know or be who I am.

Finally, to Kirsty for her love and support and for putting up with me and magic.

FOREWORD

Pete Firman has that rare quality among magicians: he has kissed a lady.

For many years I was a sleight-of-hand magician, and I noticed that magicians worldwide tend not to be very good at normal things like relationships and social skills. This is why you have to pay particular attention to Pete. Pete (and I'm probably a bit of a mentor to him, to be honest), is delightful and very, very funny, and his magic is natural and engaging and of a very high calibre. You can normally judge how good a magician's magic is by how likeable a person they are, and for that reason it's really worth paying attention to every word Pete says here.

In his Introduction, Pete suggests that you learn just a few tricks and do them well: that's very good advice. If you're the geeky guy who always wants to show people tricks, you're going to bore everyone. If you're a cool guy (or girl) who can find an occasional moment to make something disturbing or magical happen, people will be staggered. Please make sure you fall into the latter category. The hardest thing when working with magic full-time is not becoming a smug geek. Pete has avoided that, although his hair is girlish and his breath can sometimes be a little "rich."

How you cope with everyone being hugely impressed with you and thinking that you're a god is up to you. Tip from me: I'm very careful not to let it go to my head. But what Pete really teaches here are ways of shaking people's worlds up for a while, of making them momentarily question their sanity. That's a great tool to have up your sleeve, and I hope you enjoy every moment of it.

DERREN BROWN, 2006

INTRODUCTION

If you're interested in magic because on your ninth birthday Mommy and Daddy booked the ruddy-faced Uncle Fiddlesticks who not only pulled a bunny out of a hat, but also made sweets appear from pockets he'd forced you to verify were empty, and you want to know how it was done, this isn't the book for you. (Stick with the counselling – you'll get through it.)

There are no trivial, throwaway routines in *Tricks to Freak Out Your Friends*. The material in *this* book is "grab you by the balls and twist 'em" stuff. It's sick, it's rude; and while they'll say it's in poor taste, they'll want to see more, and it will blow their minds. This is a book of no-nonsense, did-you-see-that tricks. Tricks that will give you the reputation of the guy or girl who does the really weird stuff, the guy or girl who can crack their nose, take a bite out of a glass, stick a barbecue skewer through their tongue, and perform magic that *won't* be forgotten two minutes afterward. If someone bent a spoon under your nose using just their mind, had it melt in your hand, and then floated six inches off the ground, you'd take notice, wouldn't you? It's all in *Tricks to Freak Out Your Friends*, and more.

Many of the tricks in this book can be performed off the cuff, during what magic guys might call the "offbeat" – those times when people aren't expecting to see something extraordinary. The tricks are designed in such a way that the audience doesn't even know they were watching something special until it's all said and done. Of course, they may have a suspicion that you're about to do a trick when you suggest they pick a card. However, to my mind, the best and certainly most memorable magic arises out of an organic set of circumstances.

What do I mean?

Picture the scene. You and a buddy are in a café, having coffee and cheesecake, when you complain of an itchy eye. You ask whether your friend can see anything in it, pulling down your eyelid so he can get a better look. He (of course) sees nothing, but you insist that it's driving you mad. Then, in a moment of sudden desperation, you jab your eyeball with a fork and shower your companion with eye juice. And without missing a beat you say calmly, "That's better."

You can't tell me he's going to forget that in a hurry.

Why, as a trick, is it so strong? Well, first, it doesn't appear to be one – you didn't intone: "Behold! I have returned from my travels of the Far East to bring you mysteries untold!" Simply, you were in a day-to-day situation when something freaky happened. You were set up for it way in advance, but he didn't even see it coming. Sucker.

Other items in this book will convince your audience that you have "666" tattooed on a really private body part. Believe me, when you make a card melt through the solid glass window in someone's front room, you won't have to follow it up by pulling a coin from behind a small kid's ear. You'll already have them. Perform it well and your friends will remember that moment for as long as they live, and that's how powerful magic can be.

This is the best way to handle this stuff. Don't learn loads and loads and bore your audience senseless with your everlasting magic show. Be picky, learn the tricks that appeal to you, and, if necessary, prepare them in advance, so when the appropriate time comes you are all set to freak out your friends.

PETE'S RULES

Tricks to Freak Out Your Friends may be guerrilla magic, but even primates have to be prepared. Below are three golden rules you'd do well to abide by if you want to get the most from the tricks in this book.

1. Practice. This should go without saying. If while practicing a secret move or some "sleight of hand" you look like Muhammad Ali playing Jenga, you're not ready to perform it yet. Wait until your deceptive actions are invisible. Regardless of whether they understand what they saw or not, if the audience sees you do *something* you're busted. As far as they're concerned they've caught you out and you've blown any chance you had of astonishing them. Make sure you hit them where it hurts every single time by being properly prepared.

2. Never repeat a trick in front of the same audience. They'll know what's coming, and any element of surprise you had on the first occasion will have vanished along with the rug you pulled out from under them the first time you stuck a fork in your eye. Why dilute that great moment you created by doing it one more time only to receive an "Aaaahhhhh – now I see" response? Instead, say something like, "Ooof, that one takes a lot out of me," or "I've got something better here," or "Hey – I don't ask you to flip me one more burger once I've eaten, you fast-food whore!" Probably best to reserve the last response for the occasions when a) you're playing in front of suckers who work in the fast-food industry, and b) they are smaller and weaker than you.

3. Never reveal the secret. "But why not, Pete?" I hear you ask. I'll tell you why not: because they haven't spent their hard-earned cash on my little book — how dare they steal from me?! But, more to the point, it ruins the moment you've created. You wouldn't say to a child, "Hey Russell, how about that action figure Santa brought you, eh? By the way — he's not real, your mom bought it on the way home from the hairdresser." It just spoils it. And besides, you've put the time in to learn this stuff, so you've earned the right to keep it to yourself. These are *your* secrets now.

All the tricks in this book are described and depicted for a right-handed person to perform. Therefore, if you are a southpaw (left-handed), some of the moves may need to be adapted accordingly — just use your left hand instead of the right as indicated, and vice versa. Apologies for the hassle, but I read somewhere that lefties are more creative than righties so it shouldn't prove too challenging for you, smart-asses!

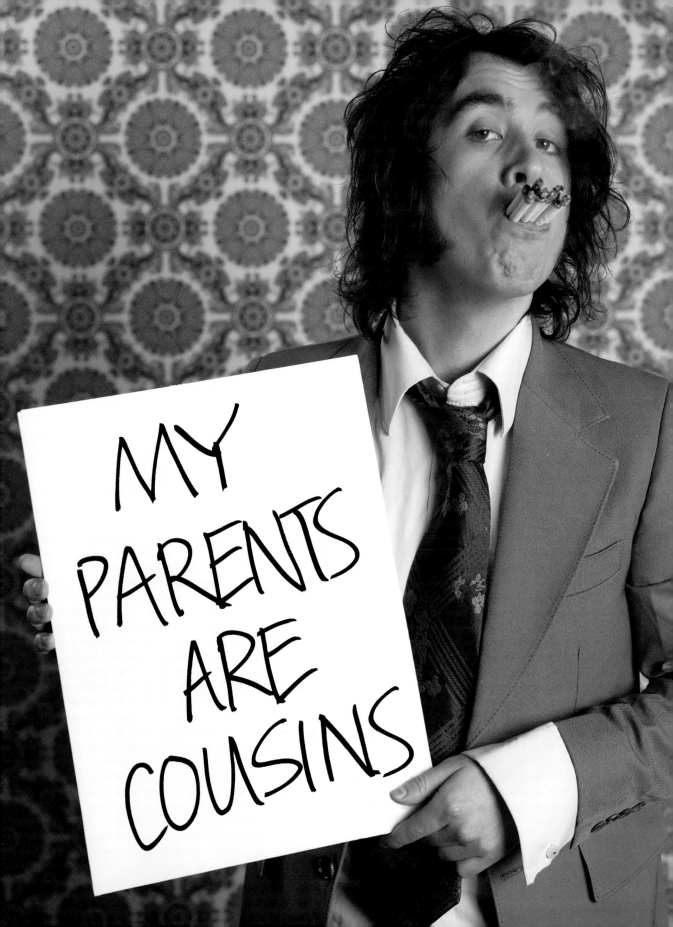

CHAPTER 1

tricks that are just plain weird

EATING FISH

So, you're at a friend's house admiring his tank full of prize-winning goldfish when you make some tasteless comment about sushi and being hungry. Your unsuspecting host laughs politely at your lame remark. Without saying another word you thrust your hand into the tank, swirl around to find the tastiest-looking specimen, snatch the squirming fella from his comfortable home, and chew him up and swallow him down faster than you can say, "Do you want wasabi with that?"

HOW'S IT DONE?

You just do it – we eat fish all the time, and eating them raw won't hurt you and they're cheap to replace.

Just kidding!

This is an old illusion I discovered when finding out about the bar magicians of Forties' America. People would meet at these bars not only to socialize, but to watch in amazement as bartenders doubled up as magicians, performing shows to earn big tips and keep the patrons drinking. They'd perform this particular trick for suckers who were sitting at the bar, where often a goldfish bowl could be found providing pretty decoration. The secret is simple.

Get yourself a big carrot and peel it. Slice a thin strip from it, and, using those age-old arts-and-crafts-tools – your teeth – nibble the slice of

carrot until it kind of looks like a goldfish. Find yourself a bowl of the orange fish and you're set to go. First, conceal the fish-shaped carrot in your right hand – casually will do – remember, no one's expecting a trick so there's no need for anything fancy. To distract them, make some heartless comment about being hungry, then stick your hand holding the carrot into the bowl and swish it around a bit. Don't scare the little fellas,

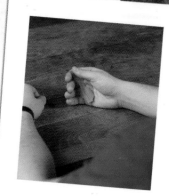

but make it look like you're really trying to catch one. Bring out your hand with the fish-carrot exposed, shake it a little as though it's wiggling and before your spectators have too long to analyze what's happening, pop the "fish" in your mouth and chew that sucker up! Swallow the lot, and conclude the performance by saying something cold-hearted like, "Mmm, it needed salt and vinegar." Believe me – they will freak out!

TOP TIPS

Make sure the bowl has lots of fish in it. If the bowl has only one occupant you ain't gonna fool Stevie Wonder with this one.

Wriggle the carrot when you pull it out of the bowl; sell the idea that you're holding a real fish.

Don't accidentally grab one of the live fish and eat it. That would be bad.

ODD DIGITS

When I was at school I was always jealous of Paul Outhwaite. He was the boy who could turn his eyelids inside out and crack his knuckles. I thought he was so cool. Paul is blind now and has chronic arthritis.

Anyway, here's a way you can crack your own knuckles (and even someone else's) without the danger of breaking their finger like a pretzel.

HOW'S IT DONE?

This one is great. The reason we squirm when somebody cracks their knuckles is because of the noise it makes, not the action. You're going to create a near-perfect reproduction of the sound of bone rubbing bone by snapping your fingers. If you are one of those losers who can't snap your fingers, skip this trick – in fact, put down this book and start

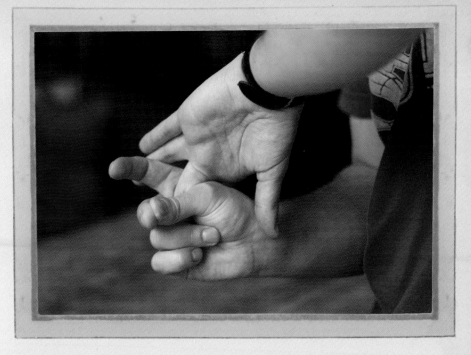

practicing now, because it's easy – it's not like I'm asking you to crack Hitler's Enigma code!

To fool your audience begin by complaining of having sore hands; perhaps make some excuse – a Greco-Roman wrestling injury or something. With whichever hand you snap best, make a fist to enclose your other hand's swearing finger (that's the middle one, dude) – my best snapping hand is my right. You are going to appear to bend your finger down hard; you can sell this by allowing your wrist to go with the movement, too. As you get to the furthest point on the downward bend, give it your best finger-snap – the backs of your hands conceal all the workings. The photo above demonstrates what's going on back there.

All that remains is for you to give a "that's better!" look and carry on as if nothing happened.

If you are feeling brave you can also perform this trick on someone else's finger – just be really careful not to get carried away with the bending. The action is exactly the same and they'll freak out as they hear the awful sound and get the visual on their own hand. However, should you do it to someone and you hear two cracks – when you only snapped your fingers once – you may have a problem. Get two lollipop sticks, some ties, and a good lawyer.

TONGUE KEBAB

My favorite place to cause mayhem is the kitchen. Think about it — the place teems with dangerous objects and appliances! One of the best gut-wrenching tricks of all time is this one, so prepare to dazzle a friend or relative with the ancient Mystery of the Kebab Skewer. Picture the scene: you reach into the cutlery drawer and grab a metal skewer (make it a clean one — tetanus is no fun). You stick out your tongue and turn to the side, and then you (apparently) stick the skewer through your tongue. They think it's the same old trick where the skewer goes behind your tongue and not through it; but then you slowly face them to reveal the shard of cold steel piercing the center of your tasting tool. Fakir them!

HOW'S IT DONE?

Behind the scenes, grab yourself a wire coat hanger, a metal file, and some pliers, because you're about to make a super-duper magic skewer. Got them? Good.

Cut the bottom from the hanger, and make sure you dull any sharp edges with a file.

Next, bend a loop into the center of the wire as shown in the photo. Finally, hide your magic skewer in the cutlery draw and wait for your moment.

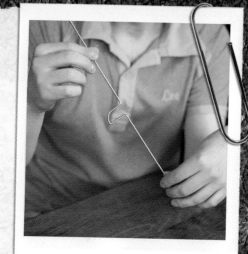

When you are ready to perform this one, take the skewer out of the drawer while making sure you conceal the bend with your right hand. Turn to your left, keeping your side to your audience, and stick out your tongue. Then, with suitable drama, pretend to pierce your tongue with the skewer as shown, while allowing it to run behind your tongue until you get to the loop. At this point push your tongue into the loop and twist the bend into your mouth. When you turn to face your audience it will look like you've really pierced your tongue, and believe me, they will react, especially if you've grimaced and grunted throughout the ordeal. Hardcore freak-outers may also consider using one of those blood capsules they sell in joke shops for the moment you turn to show them the full penetration. Matron! Have the capsule concealed in your mouth and break it just before you turn to face the horrified onlookers. The visual illusion of the skewer piercing your tongue and the dribbling blood may mean they soil themselves. Yes!

There are a couple of ways to get rid of the evidence and wrap up the trick. Reverse the procedure (hiding the bend) and put the fake skewer in your bag as soon as possible. Alternatively, quickly leave the room as if the trick's gone horrifically and messily wrong, make your way to the bathroom and hide the skewer there. Either way, get rid of the evidence as soon as possible.

Have fun with this one, it's really good!

SORE NECK

HEALTH WARNING

You meet some friends for a drink, everyone asks how everyone else is doing, and all reply with the usual "great," "fantastic," and "wonderful." Even though relationships are failing, work is depressing, and the cat just died. You explain that you're not feeling great, and that your neck is a bit sore (an old topiary accident). With that pronouncement, you grab your head with both hands and twist it sharply, and to their horror your friends hear the most painful-sounding crack of vertebrae. You move your noggin slowly from side to side and coolly reply, "That's better."

HOW'S IT DONE?

This is one of my faves – easy as pie and high impact. You need to find yourself a plastic cup, the kind they use in really shady nightclubs to make brawling that much more difficult. You may know that if you stand on one of these suckers the rim cracks with a great sound.

It's best if you're wearing a jacket for this trick. Conceal the cup inside your left armpit, under your coat, and make sure that the plastic isn't in contact with your skin as you don't want to be scratched or cut once the cup breaks. Begin by complaining of the phantom neck injury – perhaps say you once wrestled Hulk Hogan or something. Place your left hand under your chin as if you were resting it on a table, and your right hand flat on your head and forehead. You want to create the illusion of twisting your head like a demented chiropractor, but it's important you don't get too carried away and actually do it. To paraphrase Larry: "Try acting, dear boy!" Make sure you're putting pressure on the cup with your left arm and give your head a sharp twist (acting, remember!) while at the same time breaking the cup under your armpit. Timing is important on this so practice ahead of meeting your audience, with no one around.

Get it right and this is one they'll never forget.

IMPORTANT

Once again, please don't *really* twist your head – you may find yourself getting all excited and giving it a proper yank in the heat of the moment, but this is bad. Not only could you seriously hurt yourself, but *two* loud cracks makes the trick look bad.

CRYSTAL CANINES

So you've been roped into attending yet another wedding. Why can't people just live in sin? The ceremony was painful and now you're on the lawn of some stately home talking to someone who could successfully record an audiotape to help insomniacs drop off to sleep. To amuse yourself and to freak out your new "friend," you place the glass you're holding to your lips and bite a piece out of it with a loud crack, crunching the shards between your teeth and swallowing the pieces. Mr. Fascinating looks slightly worried; you merely smile and explain that you just couldn't wait any longer for the hors d'oeuvres.

HOW'S IT DONE?

This one is all sleight of hand, not sleight of mouth. You obviously don't *really* eat any glass – that would be stupid. Instead, a coin is used to create the sound of biting off a piece of glass – a quarter is perfect as it's a larger coin.

Hide it in your right hand between your index and second fingers. This puts pressure on the coin, the top of which is being held away from the glass by your right index finger.

After bringing the glass up to your lips, pretend to take a bite out of it – and, at the same time, slide your index finger up allowing the whole of the flat side of the coin to strike the side of the glass, producing the "crack" noise. Ham this up with a pained grimace to help make it believable.

The "glass" you chew on afterwards to enhance the illusion – how's that done? Easy. On the last sip of drink you had before performing the trick you also took a small ice cube in your mouth and held it there until you were ready to do the trick. After you've taken the bite from the glass, crunch up the cube, and the sound allows for the perfect illusion of you chewing up glass. Get rid of your unbroken glass by putting it on a waiter's tray as he walks past – no evidence, and you're home free. Cracking!

IS HE STILL WITH US?

What would you say if I declared I was going to kill myself? You'd probably say, "No, Pete – please don't!" But what if I said that I'm going to kill myself – and then come back to life in a matter of seconds? Have no fear, friends, I am well trained. And so will you be too.

First, I request that you kindly check my pulse – it feels normal. I ask you to shout out if that changes. I then go into a trance-like state, as if I'm watching *Oprah*. Suddenly, you notice my pulse slowing down until it eventually stops completely – I'm dead. But wait. My pulse flutters and then begins to beat as fit as a butcher's dog's. How so? Read on.

HOW'S IT DONE?

This one involves some preparation ahead of time. You need a small, hard ball like a golf or racketball. Attach a safety pin to it using some tape and pin it just under your armpit inside your jacket. Now, if you press your arm to your side you will slow the blood pressure inside the artery that runs down your arm to the point on your wrist – where the pulse is normally taken. By releasing the pressure the blood runs again and the pulse returns. The key to it is all in the presentation and the speed at

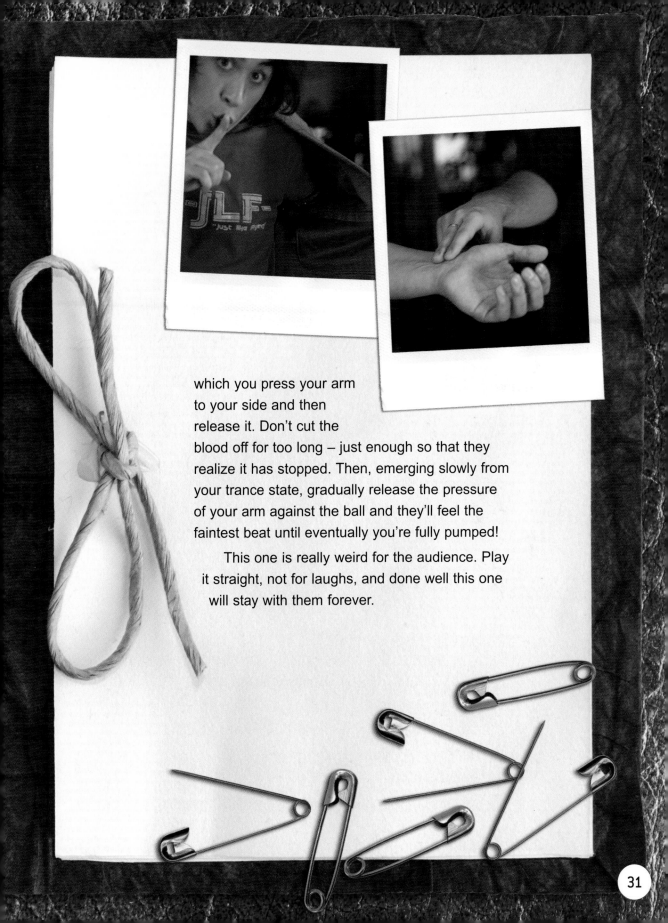

which you press your arm
to your side and then
release it. Don't cut the
blood off for too long – just enough so that they
realize it has stopped. Then, emerging slowly from
your trance state, gradually release the pressure
of your arm against the ball and they'll feel the
faintest beat until eventually you're fully pumped!

This one is really weird for the audience. Play
it straight, not for laughs, and done well this one
will stay with them forever.

CRACKING SCHNOZ!

I ask my friends if they think I have a big nose.
"Don't be ridiculous, Pete – you've just got a small face."
Thanks.

    I hope your friends will be more sympathetic; whatever they say, explain that you think your nose is crooked. It could really do with correcting and you can't afford plastic surgery, so you've decided to do it yourself. With that you grab your honker with both hands and yank it to one side. An unpleasant *crack* is heard by all, you reveal your new and improved snout and ask, "Does that look better?" They grimace so hard and for so long they all need Botox!

HOW'S IT DONE?

There are two requirements for performing this bad boy. First, you must have unchewed nails, and second, you must have teeth. If there are any toothless nail-biters reading this – how *do* you manage it?

This trick is easy. Cup your nose with both hands, and under the cover of your fingers place your thumbnail behind one of your front teeth. As you appear to wrench your nose straight, snap your thumbnail off the tooth to create the sound of cracking shnoz cartilage. The violent movement used to straighten your sniffer conceals the fingernail action and will leave your audience gagging.

HUMAN ASHTRAY

This one falls into the category I call "Geek." Back in the day, geeks weren't the guys who aced their SATs because they lacked social skills and good looks. No – the geeks were hardcore. Working in the carnivals and sideshows of Twenties America, their audience would gasp in amazement as they bit the heads off chickens and snakes and growled at the onlookers. I don't suggest biting the head off anything; however, this trick *will* have your audience squirming and gasping in disbelief.

You borrow a cigarette, light it, and get it really puffing. Then you stick out your tongue and stub the nasty illness causer out on your love licker! Does anyone have a breath mint?

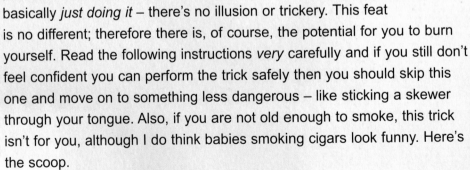

HOW'S IT DONE?

A quick disclaimer. Like many feats performed in the sideshow world, you are basically *just doing it* – there's no illusion or trickery. This feat is no different; therefore there is, of course, the potential for you to burn yourself. Read the following instructions *very* carefully and if you still don't feel confident you can perform the trick safely then you should skip this one and move on to something less dangerous – like sticking a skewer through your tongue. Also, if you are not old enough to smoke, this trick isn't for you, although I do think babies smoking cigars look funny. Here's the scoop.

To begin, light the cigarette and get it really smoking – a few large draws should do the job (no need to inhale if you don't want to). By that I *don't* mean set your mother's underwear on fire. As you are psyching yourself up to perform the feat you'll need to accumulate a good load of saliva on the surface of your tongue – it's concave anyway, so the sputum sits there nicely. The photo on the opposite page shows my puddle of spittle. Now, hold the cigarette between fingers and thumb, with the lit end pointing down, and when you're ready lift it up to your tongue and *dab* it on your tongue – *do not* push it. They should be small dabs and the audience should not be aware of them – to them it should just look like you are pressing it onto your tongue. The saliva you've accumulated extinguishes the cig surprisingly quickly; it will only require two or three dabs. You'll hear the hissing stop (the audience shouldn't hear the hissing as it's so quiet and they're usually screaming at this point) and then you can push the cigarette down in one spot.

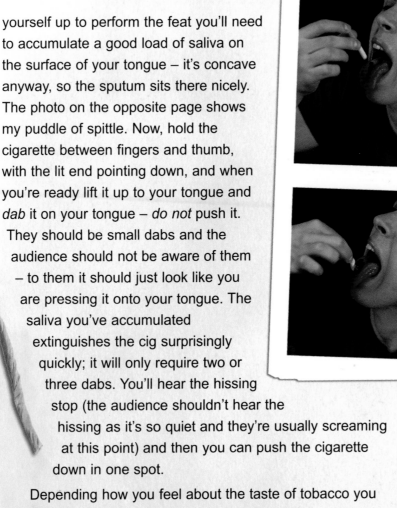

Depending how you feel about the taste of tobacco you can make this as sick or subdued as you like. Once it's gone out, I like grinding the cigarette on my tongue with lots of gagging and spluttering, but if you want to be Mr. Hardcore, just do it calmly. So, there you have it, friends. Pack your suitcase and join a sideshow – the human ashtray has arrived!

UP YOURS!

This one is perfect for an impromptu performance when you have nothing prepared. Hell, if you're naked and pressed to do a trick, this is the one you should pull out. As long as you've got hands you're good to go!

You amaze your audience by pulling off your middle finger. To prove that you've not just bent it backward, you show them your hand, front and back. Just before they scream and drop their babies you return your finger to its rightful place and show it proudly for all to see.

HOW'S IT DONE?

This one basically hinges on your ability to do a decent Vulcan Salute. If you have no idea what that is, either have a look at the photo at the top of the page or attend a Star Trek convention. Probably best to check out the photo.

To begin, hold your right hand stretched out, fingers straight, with the back of it toward your audience. The pictures on these pages show what the suckers will see. Raise your left hand to your right hand and apparently pull off your middle finger. This is done by bending the top of the right middle finger, from the middle knuckle to the tip, back, while its "disappearance" is covered by

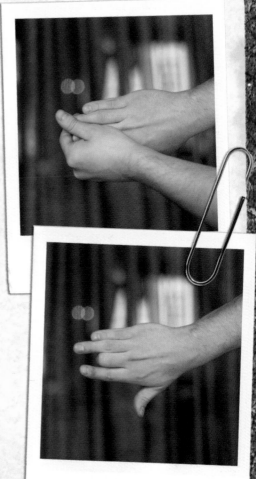

your left hand. The left comes away and is held in a fist as if it were holding the right finger, but forget about that hand for a moment and focus all the attention on your stump. The audience will see that the top of your middle finger is missing.

You are now going to show the front and back of your right hand a few times, and quickly, to show that you haven't simply bent it back – and this is where your Vulcan move comes in. As you turn your hand, baring your palm toward the crowd, straighten your middle finger and assume the Vulcan position. Hold it for a second, and, when you rotate your hand back, reverse the procedure and bend your middle finger back to its "amputated" position. Done quickly, the eye is fooled into thinking that it's seeing the same gap, front and back. Do this front and back move a few times and stop with the back of your hand toward the fools. Move your left hand (remember you appear to have been holding your "missing" finger through all of this nonsense) up to your right and cover the bent-back finger. Now, straighten it, move your left hand away and wiggle your fingers, including the one magically restored.

The whole trick is quite quick, so don't overdo it. Just say, "Hey, watch this, numbnuts, it's weird . . ."

I wish you success – live long and prosper.

I AM THE RESURRECTION

You're lounging at a barbecue, having drinks and eating meat. Inevitably, a heated conversation begins on religion. Initially, you avoid getting involved, but eventually you can't control yourself, blurting out, like some holy Tourette's sufferer, "I am the Second Coming!"

The distasteful looks and furrowed brows force you to prove your absurd claim. You locate a dead fly on a nearby window sill. Everyone can see that it's as dead as Milli Vanilli's pop career. You place the poor little fella on your paw, spout some authentic-sounding incantation, and lo and behold – the fly begins to move, walk, and eventually takes majestically to the sky. Now start your own cult, or have another burger, because you've earned it!

HOW'S IT DONE?

This one requires a bit of preparation ahead of performance, but once this is done it's easy to perform. The toughest part is catching a fly . . . alive! I've found the best way is to live in squalor and never tidy up, and if Mom complains, explain, "Hey – it's for a trick!" You want to get yourself a big one, such as a bluebottle. Once it's caught, transfer your beautiful new assistant into a small box with a lid, then place him into the freezer for a couple of hours. Yes, you heard me right – the freezer, for a couple of hours. Don't worry, this won't kill it;

instead, it slows down the fly's metabolism and makes it go into a kind of hibernation.

To prepare for your performance, get your little fella out (no, not that one) and place him somewhere in the shade. I favor a window sill as it's the kind of place you'd find a dead fly. My friend prefers the bumper of a car, notoriously the final resting place for many a bug. Wherever you choose, make sure it's out of the way and in a cool spot.

When you're ready to prove your godliness, make a big deal of searching for something in order to demonstrate beyond doubt to the audience your ridiculous "I am the Almighty" claim. Don't go straight to the fly – hunt him down. Then, when you've found him, pick the chilly fly up carefully and place him on your palm. Now, all you have to do now is your best "son of God" bit as the heat from your hand warms the fly through. You'll find it won't take very long before the little guy is moving around and then he'll fly away. Take a bow, Mr. Magic, because you just toasted their marshmallows!

IMPORTANT

This trick will succeed or fail depending on your ability to "sell" the effect. Make it as believable as you can and you will create a moment they will never forget.

IS THERE SOMETHING IN MY EYE?

This brilliant trick is the brainchild of the hilarious Las Vegas magician Mac King. Apart from having one of the best comedy magic shows in the world, Mac is also a great guy and I'm very grateful he allowed me to include his trick here.

So, you're out with your friends enjoying some food and wine in one of your hometown's finest establishments. But something's not right; you complain of an itch in your eye, though at first dismiss it. But it persists, bugging you so much that you ask one of your "friends" (read, "suckers") to have a look for you – they find nothing. In frustration at the annoying itch you pick up a fork from the table and jab it in your eye, shooting ocular juice all over your companions. "That's better," you say, wiping your face and carrying on with your meal as if nothing happened.

HOW'S IT DONE?

This messy but spectacular trick requires that you get yourself a milk or cream packet – you know, those little creamers they give you in cheap restaurants? The next time you're out somewhere that has them, grab a few or get one from the place in which you intend to perform this sick trick. Have the creamer in your lap so you can retrieve it unnoticed in a moment. And, by the way, this trick's best (and easiest) performed while seated.

Begin by complaining about your eye bothering you and generally making a fuss. Ask a friend to take a look, and help their examination along by grabbing a clean fork and using the tines to carefully pull down the lower eyelid of the "affected" eye. While all the attention is on your eye, take this opportunity to get the milk container into your unoccupied hand. Make sure the foil end of the packet is at the bottom of your fist.

Following their amateur examination of your eye, your friend will (of course) say that they can't see anything. But then – a breakthrough! Say you think you may be able to get it yourself. Bring the hand with the milk container over the soon-to-be-pierced eye as if to rub it, making sure the container is concealed in your fist from their view. Then bring up your other hand holding the fork, and carefully push the tines of the fork into the foil top while squeezing the container a little. The picture demonstrates what's happening, although obviously make sure you conceal the creamer.

With the lid pierced, the cow juice will squirt out of your fist all over your compadres! In the commotion, drop the fork to the table and move the hand with the empty milk container back to your lap. Leave it there while your friends make retching noises. Then, wipe off the milky mess from your own face and say how much better you feel. Eventually, discard the container when the reaction has calmed down – although with this belter that may take some time.

IMPORTANT

I have performed this trick many times and never hurt myself. When you pierce the container's foil lid make sure the plastic end of the creamer is against your fist, not your eye; in other words, your hand takes the pressure of the strike.

LIGHTER THAN AIR

For years, magicians have been dreaming up ways to fool us into thinking that they have powers that defy the laws of nature. We all know the trick where the tuxedo-wearing guy makes a woman float in the air – but it always lacks something. Primarily, this is because it's pretty easy for an intelligent person to reason that this type of trick can only be performed in a theater or some other controlled environment with the right technical support.

The trick I offer you now does away with all that. You, outside and in broad daylight, float from the floor into the air where you hover momentarily, then return to terra firma – without a sequin in sight. Performed effectively, this one will destroy them!

HOW'S IT DONE?

This trick relies totally on the angle from which it's viewed. Without wishing to destroy your dreams of weightlessness, you are basically going to support yourself on the tippy-toes of one foot. From where they're placed, the audience won't spot this – instead, they'll see the heels of both your feet together, off the ground, which will fool them into thinking you are floating.

To find the right position from which to do the trick is easy. And, personally, I think it's best to perform this in front of a small group of people; the larger the number, the wider they'll spread out and the greater the likelihood of their figuring out your technique. I'd say four people should be your maximum audience.

First, keep them in a tight group together and stand with your right-hand side to them – at this stage you are standing right next to them. From this position, walk forward a few steps. From the correct position, you would have to look back over your right shoulder to see your audience. Picture, from here, what they'll see – the back of your heels, while the business part that's doing the lift (the toes of your left foot) are hidden behind your right foot.

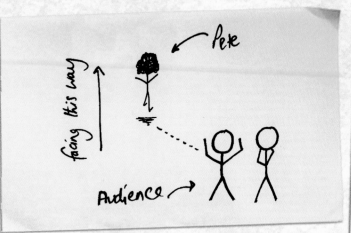

Now that you're in the correct position, prepare for the "lift." Hold your feet tightly together and outstretch your arms for dramatic effect! Lean forward slightly, putting your weight on to your toes. Now, keeping your right foot straight, parallel to the floor, and your heels tightly together, slowly lift yourself up on the toes of your left foot. The smoother you can make this movement, the better it looks. Try not to lean to one side, and keep your body as upright and balanced as you can. Once you're up there, with your right foot hovering about an inch from the ground, hold the position for a few seconds and then exactly reverse the movement to bring yourself back to the ground.

The overall effect of this trick is enhanced if you build up to performing it with some sham breathing exercises – make them think levitation's an athletic struggle. Likewise, when you come back down to earth, pretend you are exhausted. Not only does this help to make the trick believable, but being tired is a good excuse to get away with only doing it once. Crafty, eh?

DARWIN'S THUMB TRICK

I love tricks involving apparent self-mutilation as much as any other Ozzy Osbourne fan. This next nugget of magical gold allows you to appear really hardcore, but it's as safe as houses.

Simply, you cut off the end of your thumb. No magic words, no pixie dust – just plain, old-fashioned amputation.

HOW'S IT DONE?

To prepare for this trick you need to get yourself a paper napkin and a carrot with an end about the same size as your thumb – of course, the carrot can be cut down to size.

Without your audience seeing, hold the napkin with your left hand and conceal the carrot beneath it. I usually keep the whole lot in my lap until I'm ready to razzle-dazzle my peeps. Get them hooked by talking about body modification and the lengths some losers go to look cool. Have everyone check out your thumb – make them touch it. Not only

does it convince them it's real but personally I like to be touched by strangers. Now, cover your hand and thumb with the napkin (under which you're hiding the carrot) – and here, a few things happen at once. As you conceal your hand, substitute your upright thumb with the carrot; grasp the root veg with your thumb well out of the way. The photo on the opposite page (right) shows the situation with the napkin removed for clarity – I'd always recommend you use the napkin as without it the trick kind of falls short. From the audience's point of view they think they are still seeing the shape of your biggest little piggy under there.

At this point, with your "thumb" covered, go on about having a high pain threshold, mind over matter, or any mumbo-jumbo really, and then dramatically cut off the tip of the carrot with a sharp pair of scissors. *Be careful!* If you trust someone enough, have them cut it for you. Or, if you're feeling really ambitious, introduce your evil rabbit and have him chew your thumb off. The choice is yours. Wind up the trick by running to the nearest public toilet screaming your head off, and hide out there until someone comes to see how you're doing. If that takes a while, you've always got the carrot to munch on.

NASAL FLOSS

Ideas for magic tricks can strike at the most unusual of moments, so imagine my surprise when, as I bit into a quadruple cheeseburger with extra cheese, bacon, pickles, and a brass band, this little wonder arrived.

You tear the end off a drinking-straw wrapper, stick the straw in your nostril, and push the wrapper up and into your hooter. Not only that, but at the halfway-up point you begin to pull the same wrapper out of your other nostril, proving that your sinuses are weirdly connected and you are a freak.

HOW'S IT DONE?

I'll admit it up front; those of you who are blessed in the nose department will find this one easier. I can do it and I have a dainty pixie nose. They call me Cyrano.

To prepare you need two straws with paper wrappers. Tear the end from one and carefully push the wrapper down the straw – make sure you don't tear it, so be gentle.

Throw out the straw; what you end up with is a carefully bunched straw wrapper that you can conceal in your right nostril. I usually do this in the bathrooms of whichever restaurant I happen to be visiting when the desire to do this trick strikes. As long as you don't move your head around too much, the wrapper will be well hidden.

To perform this minor miracle, grab a straw from the table and tear off one end. Stick the other end in your unoccupied nasal passage and begin to push the wrapper up the straw, where it disappears up your schnozola. When it's part of the way in, begin to pull the concealed wrapper out of the other nostril, a little bit at a time. Because of the way you bunched it up there, it should pull out evenly. Also, the illusion works best if the first wrapper disappears at the same rate as the other one appears. Continue this nonsense until the wrapper on the straw is totally hidden in your nose then remove the full length of the prepared wrapper completely. Not only have you freaked them out, but you are all set to perform the trick again. Don't forget about that second wrapper though or next time you sneeze you could take someone's eye out.

CHAPTER 2

**there's no place
like home . . .
for freaking people out!**

BENDER!

Here's one I love to do at someone's house. It's just perfect for those times when you're sharing a few drinks with friends – you've had an argument over politics, each given your reasons why cannabis should be legalized, and then the moment's perfect to swing the subject round to the paranormal. You explain how people have untapped powers, that we only use 10 percent of our brains – yadda yadda!

You offer to prove your claim through a demonstration you saw on the Discovery Channel once. After your polite request, the host goes to the kitchen and brings back a handful of spoons. Each person is given one. You ask each of them to concentrate and rub . . . their spoon! Slowly, incredibly, yours begins to bend, and you gather everyone to watch your piece of cutlery, because you've managed to make the impossible happen – it bends to almost a 90-degree angle. Take the adulation, and kick back – you're getting lucky tonight!

HOW'S IT DONE?

This one has fried them all, from scientists to magicians to TV presenters. Who'd have thought this bold, *bold* trick would have made someone's entire career? OK, think now – what is the only possible way this can be done? "Urgh – you bent it when we weren't looking!"

Jackpot! However, to sum up the trick this crudely is doing it a gross disservice. The subtleties that have made this one of the most talked-about phenomena of the last fifty years are beautiful.

First, do your homework. Prior to bringing up in conversation the matter of psychic power, check the cutlery drawer, perhaps when you grab a round of drinks. You're looking for cheap, bendable stuff – if it's posh silverware, forget it. Even Israelis can't brain-bend that! Once you're confident that the tools are right, head back to the gathering, get everyone talking on the subject, and have someone go and grab the spoons.

When everyone has a spoon the psychology begins. Issue the instruction: "Hold it by the bowl and just stroke the neck."

It's vital to sell the idea that you really believe this is going to happen, because it focuses your audience on what they are doing, making them easier to distract. After you've encouraged their fruitless efforts for a while, you need to create your distraction. Perhaps, look to the person on your left and correct their technique – the way they're holding the spoon, whether it's the right way up, if they've paired vertical with horizontal pinstripe, something like that. Anything that takes the heat off you. As your right hand crosses your body to assist them, your left hand, holding the spoon, moves to your side and bends the tableware against your thigh. Everyone will be watching your assistant to make sure they're doing it right, and your deceitful action will go unnoticed.

As you assume your original position, keep the bend concealed with your flattened right hand. Begin to rub the neck of the spoon again, and, after a moment, declare that your spoon-bending appears to be working. Whereas a moment ago you "diluted focus" from your actions, at this point you want everyone to be watching you like they'd watch a man with a big rucksack on the subway. As you rub, move your fingers away so just your index and middle fingers of your left hand are left rubbing the neck. You can chuck in a beautiful illusion of the spoon actually bending itself by slowly pulling back on the bowl of the spoon with the right thumb. This causes the handle to move slowly upward. It looks great.

Hold your triumphant bend aloft to cries of amazement and consider creating a range of cheap jewelry! It's somewhat cold in print, but believe me – with enough bullshit (that's a technical term), this trick is a real reputation-maker.

GIVE ME A BREAK

This one is a great follow-up to the previous offering of metal manipulation, although it requires slightly more prep. The fools watched as you bent a spoon merely by rubbing it in a sexy but socially acceptable fashion; now, you make another spoon melt in your hands – the bowl becomes soft, droops, and eventually drops off into a spectator's clammy palm. It's fortunate you only use your powers for good!

HOW'S IT DONE?

Again, you have to do a bit of setting up. Take your spoon and bend it back and forth on the neck. It will get quite hot, so be careful. Eventually you will feel the metal getting weaker, and at this point you should make the bends smaller and less vigorous, because if you continue to wrench it the end will drop off. What you are trying to do is just to get the neck on the brink of snapping. You may destroy a handful of spoons in the process, but once you've got the knack you'll be able to do this quite quickly.

This top photograph shows the stress line on the neck, a sign that the spoon is "ready." I prepare a few spoons in this way and keep them in the inside pocket of my jacket.

While everyone is freaking out and examining the spoon that was bent in the previous routine, surreptitiously take the pre-prepared cutlery out of your pocket and move your hand to the other spoons on the floor used by your friends in the previous trick. Don't worry about it, you have plenty of misdirection – it just looks like you're picking up another spoon.

Following the success of "Bender!," you can then suggest taking the "experiment" further. I like to get close to a lady at this point – chicks dig psychic phenomena. Pre-stressed spoon in hand, rub the neck with your finger, applying a very slight pressure. It doesn't take much for the spoon to move a little. You'll feel it almost want to go. Stop rubbing the neck, and ask your groupie to cup her hands. At this point, hold the spoon at the bottom of the handle and gently shake it by way of encouragement. What you get is the illusion of the spoon drooping and then the bowl falling off into her hands. It's a killer!

Of course, the performance is also important for this trick. Don't play it for laughs, but don't be super-serious either. I like to make it appear as if I'm as surprised as they are. It also helps to throw in a little suggestion to your banter. As you rub, say something like, "Yep, this one's getting very soft – it's like butter. It's melting – look, it's just drooping and melting apart!" Once the bowl lands in their hand, ask them to check it, to make sure it's not hot, but cool. Just like you, you molecular manipulator!

MAGIC POWDER

Tricks that hint at drug abuse are always a crowd favorite. Who can forget David Copperfield's acid-tab routine? A seminal piece. This one owes a lot to Dave, a man whose greatest trick is to have the wind blow through his hair . . . indoors!

You offer to show a friend a card trick, and after their convulsions settle they choose a card and remember it. They kindly return it to the deck, which is then shuffled. You explain that to accomplish this marvellous feat of magical frippery you will need the help of some "magic powder." You sprinkle the invisible magic powder on top of the deck of cards and then proceed to apparently snort it up your nose; amazingly, at the same time, and because of your insatiable appetite for the pixie dust, you also manage to pull out a card from the center of the deck. Surprise, surprise – it's the card they had just picked. You take your applause and talk nonsense for the next three hours.

HOW'S IT DONE?

First of all, you need to have your audience member select a specific card from the pack, and this is done by "controlling" a card – that is, moving any freely selected card to the top of the deck, despite apparently mixing it somewhere in the middle. To make this demonstration of controlling easier to follow, I've marked the card that's been selected with a big black X in the photos [1]. I don't think it would be a good idea for you to do this as it kind of telegraphs what's going on.

Your friend offers you the card she's chosen. Holding the deck in your left hand, cut off half and offer the lower half to your friend on which to

5

6

7

8

place her card [2]. Place the upper half of the pack on top, but as you set the cards down put the tip of your left hand's little finger in between the two halves – this will be invisible from the front [3]. You are now going to move the selection from the center of the deck to the top in the innocent action of mixing the deck. Cut half of the cards above the break with your right hand and place these on the table [4]. Next, cut at the break you're holding with your little finger and place these cards on top of the cards on the table [5]. Finally, with your right hand pick up all the cards you are holding in your left hand (the selection is on top here) and place them on top of the cards on the table, thus bringing the selection to the top of the deck [6]. With a steady rhythm this looks like a very fair mix – I use it all the time. With the card control achieved, it's time to get on with the rest of the trick.

Pick up the deck in your left hand and hold it in a vertical position, with the selection concealed from the audience. Pretend to take some magic powder from your pocket and sprinkle it on the deck – people will chuckle because they'll think it's cute. Then lower your nose to the top of the deck and put your right index finger to one of your nostrils, which is now resting on the top of the deck [7, shown without my schnoz getting in the way]. Unbeknownst to everyone, however, your right little finger is also extended and is in contact with the back of the selection. As you sniff hard, move your right hand up, pulling the selected card out of the deck with the aforementioned little finger [8]. If you position the deck facing your audience, it will appear to them as though the card is rising out of the center of the deck [9]. When the card is about halfway out, bend back your little finger so that it doesn't give the game away, and using your right hand, pull the selection clear of the deck and hand it to your amazed audience member. If she asks you to tell her how it's done – just say no!

9

CARD ON THE WINDOW

Talk about a modern classic. This is a trick I get asked about all the time. Do it once on a group of friends and you'll nuke their heads – it's so, so funky.

The premise is great. You've had a card selected, noted, and returned to the pack, and the pack is shuffled. You then throw the deck at a nearby window, whereby all the cards but one fall to the floor. To the amazement of your beautiful assistant, her card has magically stuck to the window. You ask her to go and get it. She approaches the window, and finds to her surprise that the card is not inside the room but is in fact stuck to the *outside* of the window! Someone call a priest!

HOW'S IT DONE?

Although it appears to be a bona fide miracle, this one is actually relatively simple. You are about to learn a card move known as a "force," which is where you make a spectator choose the card you want her to have, while letting her believe she is being given a free choice. Idiots. This is necessary because ahead of the performance you'll stick a duplicate of your "force" card, from another deck, on the outside of the window.

But why don't they see it? Well, as the photo on the next page shows, the sucker – I mean, assistant – has his back to the window. In this instance I'd stuck it in plain view, knowing that my magician's chat would hold his attention. However, if you want to play it safe, you could have the card concealed by a semi-drawn curtain. This would hide the card for the majority of the trick, allowing you to move it dramatically out of the way at the same time as you throw the cards. Either way, you need to stick the card on the outside of the window.

"Forcing" a card is straightforward, once you know how. There are many variations, but they all revolve around how you display the cards for selection and the manner in which you "force" on an audience member the card you want chosen. A simple, yet sure-fire method I like is known to magicians as The Hindu Force. It goes like this.

Place the card you want picked – that is, the duplicate of the one you've already stuck to the window – at the bottom of the pack, and keep it concealed. In this instance, you want the three of Hearts to be chosen [1]. Hold the deck face-down in your left hand; grab the end of the deck closest to you with your right thumb and middle finger. Now, lift the whole pack out of your left hand with your right. With the middle finger and thumb of your left hand, you are going to repeatedly pull a few cards at a time (ten or so) from the top of the pack and drop them in your left palm [2 and 3], until your audience member calls "stop." During this "shuffling," the bottom few cards in your right hand haven't moved – the three of Hearts is still there, despite the toing and froing going on with the rest of the cards. At their call, raise the cards in your right hand so he can see the three of Hearts on the bottom, which is now his card – you've forced it on him [4]. With all the movement it appeared that the deck was well and truly shuffled, and that you couldn't have made him pick any specific card – but that wasn't the case. Once he's memorized the card, place the cards in your right hand on top of those in the left, which puts the card he just looked at somewhere in the middle.

The deceptiveness of this crafty maneuver rests on the rhythm with which you pull off the groups of cards. Done smoothly, it looks like the force card was the one he happened to stop on during your "random" mixing.

Now comes the big finish. Draw everyone's attention to the deck. Just when they're all looking and wondering what the hell you're doing, throw the cards at the window, aiming at where your duplicate is stuck on the outside. If you've played it safe make sure you move the curtain in time. Everyone will be gobsmacked that the chosen card is now stuck to the glass, but when they find out it's on the other side you will be a god!

HAUNTED KEY

This one is a stunner for budding actors, or people with the gift of the gab, as it relies on the telling of a ghost story. You produce a large iron key, originally the property of an old hotel in Peterhead, Scotland, in which you'd once stayed. The hotel was run by two strange Scotsmen who spoke in riddles, and even finished each other's sentences. You had been given room 13, and during the night of your stay, you were certain that you heard the key to your door turn in the lock – even though you knew you had locked it from the *inside*. You woke in the morning and found nothing unusual, except that the door was now unlocked. You thought nothing more of it and checked out of the hotel to catch the bus home, but it was only at the station, on reaching into your pocket to retrieve your bus ticket, that you found the room key there – although you were convinced you'd handed it in when you checked out. As a final flourish, you explain that now you always keep it with you as a memento of that strange night – and that, sometimes, in the middle of the night, you wake up startled, and can hear an old key turn in a rusty lock . . .

During the story you've handed the key around for examination, but with the tale told, you take it back and place it on your palm. You ask everyone to focus on the key to see if, collectively, you can make something strange happen. Slowly, by no visible means, the key turns over in your hand. You ask someone to pick it up straight away – they find it feels warm, but is completely free of any trickery. I've just soiled myself!

HOW'S IT DONE?

This one relies on one of magic's oldest devices – bullshit!

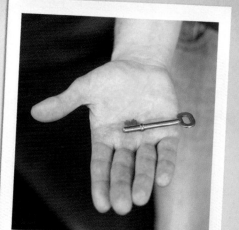

This is all about story and scene setting, and it's perfect late at night in an eerie setting. All you need is a biggish key, like the one shown in the photos. If it's old and rusty, that's even better. Decide on a story you want to use. Mine fits me, but if it fits you, too – tough; you'll have to write your own. Just kidding – use it! When you've wrapped up your spooky tale, hold the key in your hand in the position shown here. Notice that the key can freely turn in the hand. Making it move is simple. By imperceptibly opening your hand, this shifts the balance of the key and it will roll over.

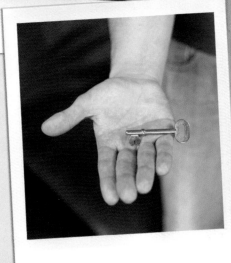

That's it, at least in basic terms. Of course, to make it look good you're going to have to practice. You'll need to find its tipping point – the place where the key will balance, yet with the slightest movement will begin to turn. The actual turn shouldn't be rushed – do it slowly. This makes it seem really creepy. Once you've performed this miracle, have your gullible audience take it from your palm and then, as if it was an afterthought, ask them if it feels weirdly warm. Of course it does, but it ain't got anything to do with ghosts or ghoulies – it's because it has been nestling in your warm hand, as well as those of others.

Don't be tempted to sell this one short. It may read simply on the page, but this one not only fools them, but also really freaks them out.

PASTEBOARD* OVERLOAD

In the mind of the dumb sucker, most card tricks all look very similar, however impressive they may actually be, and this realization led me to eliminate all the weaker, more convoluted ones from my repertoire. This trick is definitely *not* one of those. It looks really flashy and skillful but is actually quite simple. Traits that, incidentally, I look for in most of my material and women.

An audience member selects a card and returns it to the deck, which is then shuffled. To make it impossible for you to manipulate the cards, you put them back in the box. Suddenly, you throw the box into the air and catch it in your left hand. The audience nearly collapses as the selected card has appeared in your right hand!

Now, who's for poker?

HOW'S IT DONE?

To perform this artifice with a deck of cards you need to be familiar with "card control," explained in the trick "Magic Powder." It's also important that your card box has a semicircle cut out at the lid — if it hasn't already got one, feel free to chop one in yourself, assuming they're not your granny's beloved Golden Jubilee limited-edition set, that is.

Get a sucker to choose a card and return it to the pack, and

60

then skillfully control it to the top of the deck using the "Magic Powder" method. Place the cards back in the box, ensuring that the "selection" (the card chosen) is closest to the cut-out. Now, as you close the lid, place the lid flap between this card and the rest of the deck. This allows the selection to be pulled free of the case without the lid holding it in. Hold the box in the way shown, and with your thumb on the back of the card, pull it up slightly so you can grip it with your finger. Now, throw the box into the air while holding on to the selection. The deck spins upward and everybody's eyes follow it. Catch it in your left hand and look back to your right hand, and react suitably to the card that has mystically appeared there. Your audience will toss their children up in the air in celebration!

* "Pasteboard," by the way, is an old word for a playing card. Numbnuts!

POKER FACE

Inevitably, once someone knows you dabble in the dark arts he will fall over himself to demonstrate his "great" card trick. You know the kind of thing. A terrible trick he struggles to remember while performing it, which he invariably messes up, and, if by some miracle he manages to get it right, it's very often crappy and not worth the effort.

It's at that moment I like to take the cards from him, and, with a couple of flashy moves, cause the four aces to leap from the deck in a death-defying display of sleight-of-hand conjuring! Try not to rub in the fact that you've just obliterated your amateur magical friend – laughing in his face should be sufficient.

HOW'S IT DONE?

I'll be honest, friends – this one's a toughie that requires lots of practice to make it look slick. However, once you've got it down it's a killer demonstration of your expertise with a deck of cards. The trick involves producing four aces out of the pack in quick succession – despite the deck apparently being mixed throughout with various cuts (destroying any theories of the cards being under your control). However, only *you* know that these aces are in very specific positions that allow them to be "magically" plucked out and presented to your waiting audience. Once you've mastered it, perform it as fast as you can for maximum effect.

To begin, start with three of the aces on the top of the deck and one on the bottom. The audience should be unaware of this preparation, so ideally do it out of sight. If that's not possible, arrange the aces into their positions while nonchalantly running through the cards – ensure only you can see the faces, obviously. Done casually it looks like you are just mixing the cards, and remember that nobody has a clue what you are about to do anyway!

Holding the deck from above with your right hand, lift up approximately half of the cards with your right index finger and move them to the left [1]; they will pivot at the back on your right thumb. Take this top section of cards with your left hand and place them in the crotch of the left thumb. Now, move the wad of cards in your right hand (at the bottom of which is a single ace) on top of those in your left hand, ensuring your left thumb makes contact with the ace at the bottom. With your thumb, pull the ace to the left and pivot it along the side of the deck up and on to the top of the deck, face up. Thus, the first ace mysteriously appears [2]. Place the ace on to the table in front of you with your right hand – one down.

When you appeared to combine the two halves of the deck (as described above), you actually maintained a break with your left little finger, at the back, between these two halves [3] – this couldn't be seen from the front because of the pressure from the left fingers at the front, which closed the gap. This break will help you reveal the second ace. Cut the cards above the break and put them on the table. Now, move the remaining half (previously at the bottom) on top of the half on the table. The situation – unknown to the viewers – should be that there are now three aces at the top of the deck.

The second ace will make its appearance by apparently spinning out of the deck. Hold the deck by its right-top and bottom corners (backs toward you) using your middle finger and thumb. You are going to pull down with your right index finger on the top card (the ace) to create a spring in the card, which, on releasing your finger, causes the pasteboard to spin upward and away from the deck [4]. You'll need to catch it in your left hand, too! This is a very showy move that is quite tricky, but with plenty of practice you'll get used to applying the correct amount of pressure necessary to spin the card.

5

If you're still with me, well done – we are two aces down, and two to go! Place your second ace on the table next to the first.

The top two cards in the deck in your right hand should be aces. Now, despite apparently cutting the cards completely randomly, you are going to move one ace from the top of the deck to the bottom, while at the same time keeping the other ace on top – again, making it seem that you are mixing the pack. Discreetly place your left little finger under the top card (an ace) [5] and with your right hand approach the deck and grab half of it from above, maintaining the break previously held by the little finger with your thumb. Don't present the cards side-on to your audience in the way they are shown in the photo – it simply demonstrates the break more clearly [6]. Move the cards remaining in your left hand on top of those in your right, still holding the break between the aces [7]. Finally, cut all the cards *below* the break with your left hand and move them to the top of the deck. You will have now positioned one ace on the top of the pack and another on the bottom – well done, you!

6

7

It's time for the big finish. Hold the cards in your left hand with your fingers underneath the deck and your thumb on top. With an abrupt movement, throw the deck to your right hand, but keep your fingers on the ace on the bottom and your thumb on the ace at the top. You'll find the deck flies out from between these two cards to be caught by your waiting right hand [8]. To your amazed onlookers, it appears as though the two aces were magically plucked from the center of the deck – your speed has fooled them all.

And that's it. What has taken so many words to describe is performed at a swift pace, and it's one of those wham-bam-thank-you-ma'am tricks that will definitely impress [9].

8

9

SUPER-SWEET COIN VANISH

I was introduced to this one by my manager at one of our meetings (he says nice things about me when I'm feeling down). I knew I had to include it in this tome as it tore my balls off.

You show a coin on your outstretched palm, wave your other hand over it, and the wee doubloon disappears!

HOW'S IT DONE?

First off, you need to consider what you're wearing (for once). Slip into a jacket with open sleeves, as the coin shoots up there. There are no wires or other tricks here – it flies up your sleeve under its own momentum. Hold the coin on your flattened left palm, which should be held at about forty-five degrees to the floor. Your hands are going to move quickly toward each another, with the left hand holding the coin moving swiftly in the direction of your open sleeve. As the right covers the left, your left hand will sharply stop its motion, which will propel the coin into your right sleeve. Wait a beat as if "making the magic happen," then separate your hands to show how the coin has vanished. The larger and heavier the coin, the easier this is to do – less movement is needed to shoot it up your sleeve. The action of your hands coming together should look like you are waving your right hand over your left in a magical fashion (whatever that is).

The trick's not easy and it'll take some time and practice to make it look smooth. Once perfected, however, you'll have a trick you can perform at any time. Assuming you're wearing clothes.

RIP OFF

I love the kind of trick where you do all the preparation ahead of time, so that when you're ready to spring the thing on someone, all you have to do is "sell" it, winding them up until they break like a twig! This is one such trick.

Your friend has left you alone in his newly decorated room; on his return, you apologize desperately for your clumsiness and draw his attention to a nasty rip in the wallpaper. He goes mental – not because of the damage to the wall, but from the damage that his girlfriend is going to inflict on his nuts. You draw the deceit out for as long as you can before putting him (and his nuts) at ease, admitting it's just a trick. You are evil!

HOW'S IT DONE?

This one is simpler than an inbred baby that's been dropped on its head. All you need is a sheet of plain paper and some blue tack. Fold the paper in half and tear out a triangle shape through both halves of the paper, making the fold the base of the triangle. Tear the paper roughly as these edges should look like the torn wallpaper. Done correctly, on unfolding the triangle you should have a vague diamond shape – isn't symmetry cool! Roughly concertina-fold *one* of the triangles; this will be the piece that hangs off the wall. When your buddy leaves you alone (fool), stick the other triangle to the wall using a small amount of blue tack so that the concertinaed piece hangs forward. Done well it should look like a large rip in your buddy's Laura Ashley décor. Only put him out of his misery when he looks like he might cry. Don't you just love magic?

PICK ME UP

This one is a weird combination of strength and suggestion – and, to be honest, I'm not quite sure how it works, but it does. You ask a fella to sit in a chair with his feet together and hands in his lap. Four helpers clasp their hands together and extend their index fingers – two place their hands under his knees, and two under his armpits. The aim is to lift the sitting duck using just their fingers. On their first attempt, they'll achieve precisely nothing – it's just not possible.

This is where the magic comes in. With your inspiring and compelling words, they'll try again – and up the gentleman flies. This one truly baffles people because *they* do the magic and are still amazed as to how it works!

HOW'S IT DONE?

I honestly don't know, but here's the practical side. The helpers must follow the rules of the trick – and the most important part is how they hold their hands; clasped together, with fingers outstretched, as though they're firing a crap finger-gun. Now, have your monkeys put their fingers in the bend of the guy's knees and under his armpits. Make sure you haven't picked someone with a personal hygiene problem as your helpers may need a wet wipe after this one. At this stage, ask everyone to try to lift the guy. Emphasize the impossibility of the attempt because they are just using their fingers. They'll attempt the lift, and sure enough – trust me on this – they will be unable to do it.

Make some room for the magic guy! Instruct everyone to stack their hands in turn on top of the liftee's head, and to press them gently down. Explain how you are going to count to ten, and that on "ten" they are to assume their original positions and lift the man straight up in the air. Emphasize that even though a moment ago they couldn't lift the hefty fella, this time, on the count of ten, they will suddenly each have the strength of a bear and lifting him will be no problem. You count to ten, everyone lifts him, and they are astonished. Don't let this on, but the chances are that you will be too!

I've seen this done so many times, and each time it works, and I think it probably has something to do with perception and suggestion. You assume it would be impossible to lift a fully grown man using just index fingers, but remember that four people are combining their strength. Also, the first attempt is "tainted" by the fact you tell them it's impossible and can't be done, even before they give it a try – you are planting unhealthy mental seeds. After the hands-on-head-and-counting-shtick you are more positive and encouraging.

You are probably reading this thinking, "Come on Pete, pull the other one!" Honestly, try this once and you'll pull it out of the bag at every wedding reception for the rest of your life!

THE RICE AND KNIFE MYSTERY

This is perhaps the weirdest trick in the entire book. It's a challenge that is total nonsense, means nothing to most people, and that's exactly why I love it!

You fill a jar with rice and challenge your friends to lift the jar using just a knife. One condition — they can't touch the jar either with their hands or the knife. How the hell . . . ?

HOW'S IT DONE?

My psychic powers are telling me you are foaming at the mouth to get the low-down on this bad boy! The kind of jar you use is important; you need one that is wider in the middle than it is at the mouth; the knife should be a regular table knife. Fill the jar to the brim with ordinary white rice, and offer up the challenge to all takers. Once you've watched a member of your clueless audience wave the knife ineffectually at the jar, getting more and more frustrated about what to do, pry the knife from his useless fingers and ask him to observe, carefully.

Grab the knife and do your best Tony Perkins impression, stabbing it into the rice rapidly. Do this for about a minute, initially with deeper jabs, working up to shallow stabs. What you are doing is compacting the rice. When the minute's up, slowly push the blade into the center of the jar, almost to the bottom. You will find that the rice

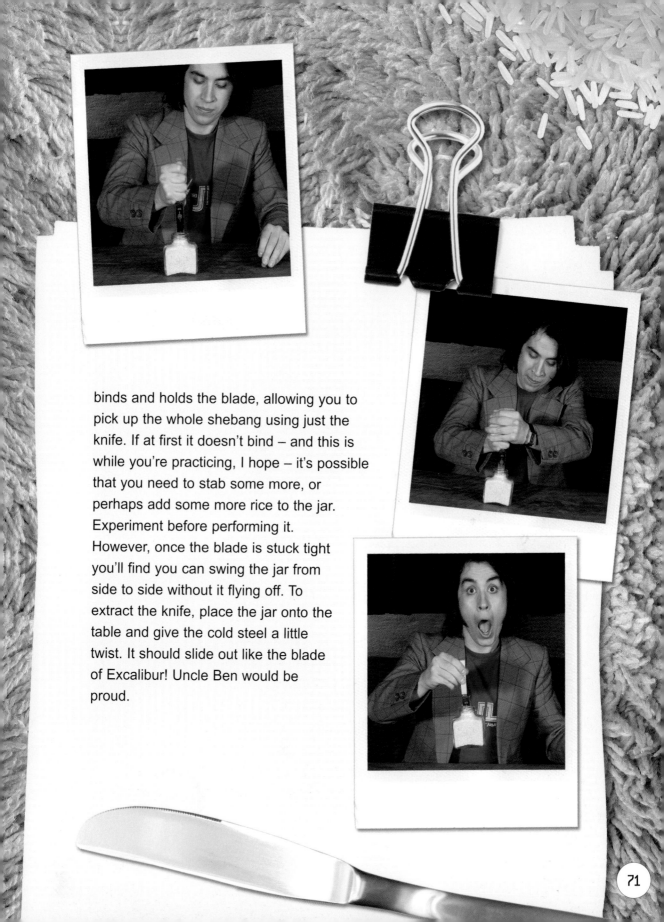

binds and holds the blade, allowing you to pick up the whole shebang using just the knife. If at first it doesn't bind – and this is while you're practicing, I hope – it's possible that you need to stab some more, or perhaps add some more rice to the jar. Experiment before performing it. However, once the blade is stuck tight you'll find you can swing the jar from side to side without it flying off. To extract the knife, place the jar onto the table and give the cold steel a little twist. It should slide out like the blade of Excalibur! Uncle Ben would be proud.

THROUGH THE EYE OF A NEEDLE

Tricks where you challenge a friend to do something at which he is bound to fail are great. On so many levels too – you not only get his embarrassment, but usually the free drink on which the bet was agreed on. This is another of those little beauties for your arsenal.

You bet the chum(p) that you can make a large coin pass through a small hole in a piece of paper. You pierce the paper, place on the coin, and – *voilà* – it passes through. Not only do you win the bet, but with a small supplementary wager you clean him out by then demonstrating that you can also push a *glass* through the small hole. Whoo-ha!

HOW'S IT DONE?

To do this you will need a piece of paper and a coin. I make the hole in the paper by folding it in half and tearing a hole that is clearly smaller than the coin I intend to push through it. At the same time, you can't do this trick with a tiny pinhole; it should just be smaller than the coin that you're using. After your viewer has admitted defeat, fold the paper in half again and have the coin "sit" in the hole at the bottom along the fold. It's obviously too big to fall through, but you'll find that if you carefully pinch the paper and lift up the sides, the coin will slip through without tearing it.

The second bet – in which you insist you can push a glass through the same hole – is magnificent. All you have to do is get a pen or pencil, stick it through the hole and push the glass with it! You see what I did there? You push the glass *through* the hole! Genius.

PIT STOP

You'll either love this or think, "Hey Pete – this sucks ass." But it's in my book because *I* think it's cool, and I'm sure you will too. It's a weird anatomical challenge, which is good to pull on people at short notice.

You challenge someone to bend their thumb into the palm of their hand. They do it easily. You offer double or nothing and they agree – after all, this is easy! Your one condition is they have to follow your instructions. They do so, but find that

every time they try to move their thumb into their palm a sharp pain runs down their arm. You just doubled your cash, *and* got to see them squirm!

HOW'S IT DONE?

I'm not entirely sure. But once you've got them to bend their thumb into their palm (as in the photograph below-left), then have them move their hand under their armpit, they'll find it impossible to straighten their thumb and then bend it back to how it was. I think this is because of the way the tendons are stretched in this position – regardless, they'll feel a sharp pain and give up in no time. Wimps!

CHAPTER 3

like nuts and chips, these
tricks go perfectly with
a few brewskis!

THE WORLD'S STRONGEST FINGER

How many times have you wanted to pierce a matchbook on the end of your finger as it was flying through the air? None? Well, it doesn't matter because once you've read the following and put in a bit of practice, you'll be impaling stuff like it ain't no thing, Vlad!

HOW'S IT DONE?

This one is a little tricky. To prepare, you need two identical matchbooks. However, it's best performed at a bar where they have a bowl of books, because this looks more organic to the sucker – er, I mean, spectator. Secretly squirrel away a matchbook and head to the bathroom or somewhere private. Once there, make a hole in the book that is large enough for you to poke the tip of your index finger through. Pull the matches out of the sides of the book so that at the reveal later on it looks as though you've pierced it with some force. Pop the prop in your right pocket and head back to the bar.

At this point let the conversation flow a little, and, as you're talking, reach into your pocket ostensibly to grab a pack of

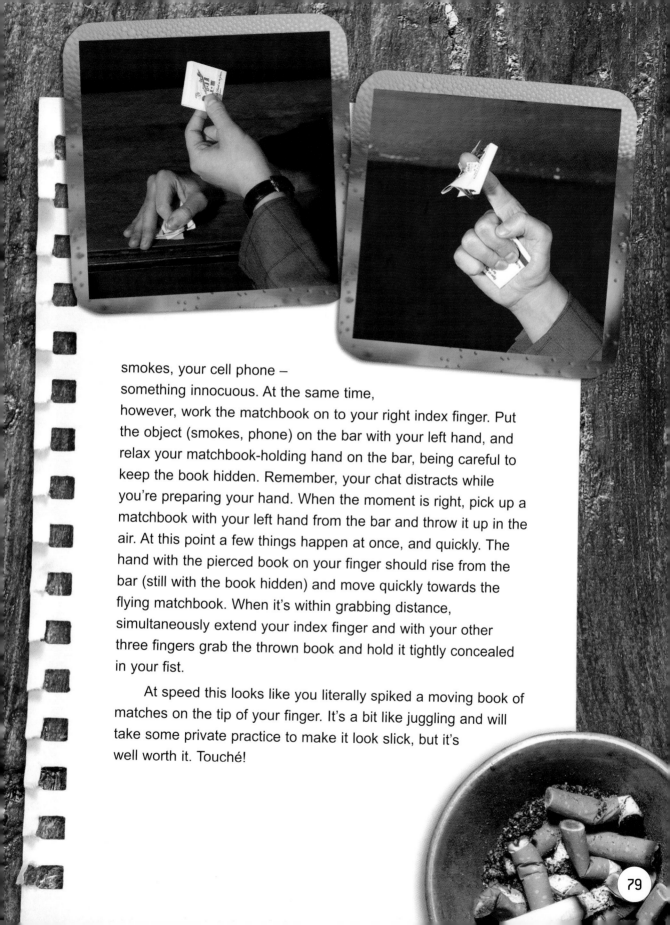

smokes, your cell phone —
something innocuous. At the same time,
however, work the matchbook on to your right index finger. Put
the object (smokes, phone) on the bar with your left hand, and
relax your matchbook-holding hand on the bar, being careful to
keep the book hidden. Remember, your chat distracts while
you're preparing your hand. When the moment is right, pick up a
matchbook with your left hand from the bar and throw it up in the
air. At this point a few things happen at once, and quickly. The
hand with the pierced book on your finger should rise from the
bar (still with the book hidden) and move quickly towards the
flying matchbook. When it's within grabbing distance,
simultaneously extend your index finger and with your other
three fingers grab the thrown book and hold it tightly concealed
in your fist.

At speed this looks like you literally spiked a moving book of
matches on the tip of your finger. It's a bit like juggling and will
take some private practice to make it look slick, but it's
well worth it. Touché!

SNORTING CIGS

This one is a classic but never fails to get a reaction. What your audience see is you borrowing a cigarette from someone, pushing it up your nose, and then pulling it out through your mouth. You then nonchalantly place the offending sinus traveller back in your friend's packet and shake it up for a fun little game of Russian Roulette!

HOW'S IT DONE?

This one appears simple but I've seen so many people mess it up. To do it well you'll have to put in a bit of practice.

Hold the cigarette at one end, cover the filter tip with your fingers so that only the white portion is seen by the audience, and press the other end against the inner side of your nose, at a 45-degree angle. It's important that you have something to push the cigarette against (i.e. the inner side of your nose) as you don't really want the horrible thing going up your schnoz. While you are (apparently) thrusting the cigarette into your honker, you actually push your fingers along in front of it; the cig runs along the inside of your middle finger. With practice the illusion is perfect. Remember, hide the filter tip from your audience right from the beginning of the trick because if it's seen the illusion of the cig entering your schnoz wouldn't work as they'd spot the filter disappear into your hand.

Once the cigarette is seemingly up there, give a couple of big sniffs as if inhaling it all the way in. Now, to make it appear from your mouth, move the hand concealing the cig to your lips and pinch it between them as you make a blowing sound, as though pushing it through your sinuses. Draw your fingers down along the cigarette as if you're pulling it from your mouth, and when you get to the end, pull it away from your lips. Again, if it's not a rolled cigarette pull it from your mouth *before* you get to the filter paper, and conceal that behind your fingers.

I like to finish it off with the Russian Roulette gag mentioned above as it gets an extra "urgh!" in an already pretty gross trick!

NICOTINE ON THE ROCKS

This trick looks so cool and impressive that people will think you are truly blessed with magical powers. You show two unprepared, ordinary wine glasses, and into one you carefully blow cigarette smoke. Amazingly, the smoke does not spill out but stays in the glass, filling it up as if it were a liquid. The big finish comes when you pour the smoke from one glass to another. After having demonstrated your clear superiority you blow into the glass, causing the smoke to disperse and proving you are way cooler than all of your friends.

HOW'S IT DONE?

I'm no science guy but I believe this one works due to the fact that the smoke in the glass is denser than the air in the glass, and therefore it sits at the bottom.

To make it a little easier you should use wine glasses with fairly straight sides. Take a big drag on your cigarette and hold the smoke in your mouth. Bring the glass up to your lips as if you were taking a drink. Now, slowly open your mouth and allow the smoke to roll into the glass, but don't blow it in as it'll just disperse back out. You'll find the smoke fills the bottom portion of the glass and will sit there quite happily. It looks awesome.

To pour the smoke from glass to glass, carefully pick up both glasses and touch them gently together so that there's no gap between them, with the smoke-filled glass slightly overlapping the empty one. Very carefully, tip the smoke from one glass to the other. You'll find it will roll into the empty glass and lay at the bottom.

I like to finish off this little number by blowing into the glass and watching the smoke blow out. Slick.

ASHTRAY MESSIAH

This little peach takes a card trick and lifts it up a notch into the realms of the bizarre. Performing this baby is like dancing with demons!

You ask a friend to choose and remember a card. The selection is returned to the pack and the deck is set down. You offer to show your audience something weird, begin to undo your jeans, and realize that maybe that's inappropriate. Instead, you roll up your sleeve to expose your forearm. Your buds look unimpressed and wonder what the hell you are doing. You then rub some ash from a nearby ashtray on your forearm and shapes begin to form. More ash reveals, astonishingly, the number of the card they just looked at! So bewildered are they that they strip you and check your whole body for the marks of Satan!

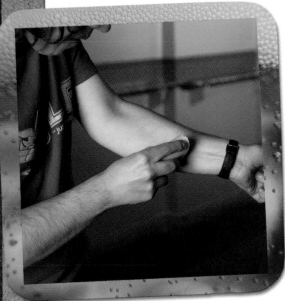

HOW'S IT DONE?

So, you draw a pentagram in chalk on your bedroom wall, sacrifice a monkey, and chant "Lucifer is lord" three times.

Just kidding, it's only a card trick. But a good one. You need to be able to force a card to perform this. I hope that you have learned this skill from performing "Card on the Window"; if you haven't mastered it and just skipped ahead because you liked the photos on this page – shame on you! Go back and learn how to force a card and then come back to do this trick.

To the rest of you – I'm sorry about that. There's always someone ready to spoil it for others.

You'll also need a bar of plain white soap. With a sharp knife, and observing all safety precautions, carve the soap in such a way that you create a point you can write with – "whittle" it, if you will. Ahead of the performance, you will use the whittled soap to write, on your inner forearm, the name of the card you are going to force. Generally, I write the number and the suit symbol. You are now all set, so grab your cards and make sure there is an ashtray with plenty of ash handy.

Force the card that matches the card written on your forearm – the trick isn't as good if they aren't the same. Roll up your sleeve and rub some ash over the prepared area. You'll find that some ash will stick to the soap and the rest will rub away; you will be left with a big, bold image of the spectator's card. They will freak out – your eyes will roll into the back of your head as you leave to play your Marilyn Manson records backward.

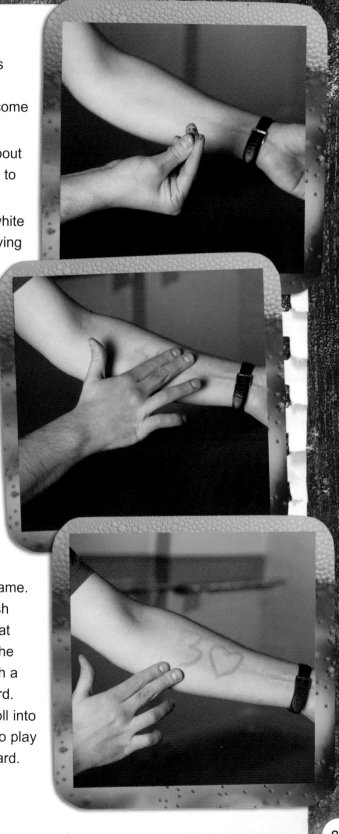

SKIN TIGHT

This is perhaps one of the prettiest tricks in this book – a complete contrast to the other dirty, filthy stuff. I had to include it as it's so magical and it freaks people out on a totally different level.

You take a cigarette paper from a packet and openly tear it up. Rolling the pieces into a little ball, you give them a magical blow and on opening the cig paper the crowd finds it is completely restored. And, guess what? Your hands are otherwise empty – no little pieces, no hidden papers. Check that, player!

1

2

HOW'S IT DONE?

To prepare for this one pull a cigarette paper from your pack and crumple it into a ball [1]. It is now to be hidden under the flap of the cigarette paper pack until you need it later – this helpful photo demonstrates, just so [2].

At performance time, take the pack from your pocket and open the flap. Pinch the balled up paper between your right index finger and thumb, behind the pack's flap; it will be totally concealed in this position. With the same finger and thumb, carefully pull another paper from the pack, give it all the gab and, using both hands, tear it up – still hiding the

previously rolled-up ball between right index finger and thumb (as above).

Collect together the pieces using your left index finger and thumb. Bring your hands together, and use the right finger and thumb to press the torn pieces in the left hand together [3]. In the action of apparently tightening the torn ball, however, you are actually swapping the two items over – the rolled-up ball from the beginning has passed to the left index finger and thumb, and the ripped-up pieces move to the right hand. The net effect is while it looks like you are screwing up the torn pieces, you are secretly substituting them for the restored piece – all in a matter of seconds. With the torn pieces hidden between your pinched right finger and thumb, all that's left to do is carefully straighten out the restored piece and take your applause [4].

To get rid of the torn pieces I just crush the restored piece in my right hand and secretly add the torn ball to it, throwing the whole lot in the bin.

BREAKING THE HABIT

Every magician knows that if you can do magic with an object borrowed from a friend or audience member it makes the trick stronger. This one fits into that category. After borrowing a cigarette from someone, you tear it in half, but with just a little magic rub, that tube of dried leaves is as good as new. You hand it back and go about your day.

HOW'S IT DONE?

You'll need what we magic guys term a "gimmick" to perform this one. A gimmick is a prop used to accomplish a trick, and one which the audience is mostly never aware of. In this instance the gimmick is a section of the white portion of a cigarette, about one-and-a-half inches long.

To begin the trick you need to get the gimmick into your left hand. I usually keep it in my left jacket pocket and grab it as I put my hands in there while hunting for a cigarette. After not finding one, ask someone if you can borrow one of theirs, and at the same time bring out the gimmick concealed in your left hand. Try not to pay this hand (or the gimmick in it) any attention – if you don't, neither will your audience.

1

Take the borrowed cigarette in your right hand, holding it by the filter tip. Bring both hands together and line up the gimmick with the end of the real cigarette [1]. Push the gimmick against the cigarette, forcing the cigarette "deeper" into

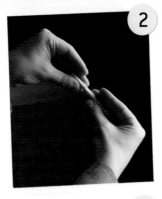

the palm of your right hand and gradually exposing the gimmick itself [2]. This movement should not be obvious to the audience, and only take a couple of seconds. Now that the "join" (where cig and gimmick meet) is between your hands, you are going to appear to rip the cig in two, but really you're just separating the cig and the gimmick. As you apparently tear the cancer stick in half, your left hand moves forward and your right moves backward. You'll have to act this a little, as adding a bit of pressure as you separate the pieces will make them rub together with a nice sound. Because it's your left hand that moves forward, the audience see most of the gimmick thinking it's a torn end, while the real (and intact) cig is safely concealed at the rear [3].

To restore the cig, explain that you need a bit of static electricity to fuse the pieces back together. To generate this, you're going to rub one of the pieces on your elbow [4]. Raise your right hand (containing the real cigarette) to the side of your head, but be careful not to let people see the whole of the cigarette. Rub the gimmick on your right elbow. Repeat this on the other arm, rubbing the end of the real cigarette on your elbow, only this time when your gimmick is up near your head drop it down the back of your collar [5]. No one will see this as you are holding the attention with your elbow rubbing. Bring your right and left hands together with the backs of your fingers toward the audience; remember to act as if you're still holding one piece of cigarette in your left hand. Work the cig in your right hand over to the left with your thumbs. Once centered between your hands, open up your fingers to show how the cigarette is restored [6]. Praise Jesus!

DRINK AS I DRINK

At the bar it's the usual story — your buds have got more brew in them than brains. You offer an easy game to decide who buys the next round, which could come in at double figures since you have visitors from London who insist on drinking Mojitos!

You explain to the big fish that if he can copy everything you do, you'll buy the next round; if he can't, he'll need to start digging deep. He fails. You win. Easy-peasy.

HOW'S IT DONE?

Start simple. You pick up your glass, he does. You toast him, he toasts you. You drink, he drinks. You toast him again, he returns the favor. You drink, he drinks. You pause and spit your mouthful of booze back into your glass. He will have swallowed his poison so will be unable to complete his task and be bound to buy the whole motley crew "just one more." This one has kept me in free drinks for a long time. Remember, never assume too much!

"But Officer, she looked eighteen!" Ouch.

MATCH THAT

If you are in a bar, feel the time is right to make some magic but find your pockets empty, this trick is perfect. It is probably my favorite bar trick.

You ask your companions whether they would like to see some magic – they say "yes." Damn it, you weren't expecting that. Not one to be thrown, you pull out a book of matches, open it up, and have someone tell you what color the heads of the matches are. He replies "red." No shit, Sherlock. You pull out a match from the book, strike it, and place the matchbook in some loser's hand for safekeeping. The match burns for a moment, and then you blow it out – and in the twinkling of a magician's dummy eye it disappears. You ask the matchbook holder to open up his guarded gift where he finds, to his amazement, that the match has returned to the stapled book. How does he recognize that it's the same match? Well, it's burnt, of course! How do you like those apples, hot stuff?

HOW'S IT DONE?

I love this trick because you can prepare it at a moment's notice. You'll need two matchbooks, readily available in the sort of establishments I frequent. If you can't find any in your local bar, skip this trick and look for the pork scratchings routine on page 203. When no one's around, or you're off on one of your now frequent trips to the toilet, strike one of the matches – still in the book – using the striking surface of the other book [1]. Careful you don't set them all off, skin grafts are not a good look.

OK – and here's the trick – now bend the burnt match down and out of the matchbook (without removing it) and close the cover. You'll find that if you hold the book and place your thumb over the turned-out match, this will conceal it [2]. This is your start position, so while your hand is in your pocket hide the match as described and pull out the book. Open it up (still holding on to the match with your thumb – it doesn't work so well if it pops up and says hello) and ask the audience to tell you the color of the match heads – this is important because the big reveal at the end depends on them noticing a difference. Now rip out a match close to the bent one you have under your thumb.

At this stage close the book, but not before bending the burnt match up and quickly pushing it into the pack with your thumb without anyone seeing. Strike the pulled-out match and give the matchbook to someone to hold. This is a great position to be in as you are now set for your big finish. The matchbook is in the possession of your volunteer, and everything is as it should be as far as they are concerned.

3

4

Blow out the match and place it on the table in front of you, close to the edge. To vanish it you are going to appear to pick it up off the table with your right hand, place it in your left, and have it disappear. What actually happens is that you let the match fall into your lap as you apparently pull the match off the edge of the table into your right hand [3]. So, hold your right hand in such a way that suggests you are holding the match, and appear to place it into your left hand – then snap your fingers, say a magic word, do a dance – whatever. Open your hands and show that the match has vanished [4]. Finally, draw everyone's attention back to the matchbook being held by your "volunteer," have them open it slowly, and show everyone that the match has, by magic, returned to the book [5]. This one is so good, I almost wish I'd kept it quiet. I must really love you.

5

IN THE PALM OF HIS HAND

Having things appear in Mr. Magic's hands are all well and good, but when you can make something appear in someone else's hand and not get arrested, you know it's a belter of a trick. This was one of the first tricks I learnt when I got into magic. You have a participant make his hand into a fist, and then you rub some cigarette ash into your palm until it dissipates and vanishes. You then tell your "friend" to slowly open his hand where, to his surprise, he finds the ash has magically appeared on *his* palm. You, my friend, should pack up and join a frickin' circus!

HOW'S IT DONE?

First, this trick is one to save for the bar. You need ready access to cigarette ash, and the abundance of ashtrays in such establishments means you can spring this bad boy at a moment's notice. While your victim is away from the table, either in the bathroom or buying you another mocktail, dip your right middle finger into the ashtray and get a good ashy covering on its tip. Now relax. Sit tight. You're all set.

On his return, keep him entertained with mindless chat for a bit, and then offer to demonstrate something weird. Ask that he holds out his hands, palms down. This, now, is the crucial part – encourage him to hold his hands "a bit closer," and as you say this take his hands and gently pull them forward, at the same time touching your ashy middle finger into his left palm. Sneaky, eh?

Move your hands away, making sure he doesn't see your dirty finger, and ask him to make his hands into fists. Ask him if he is right- or left-handed. If he says right you say, "Put that one down, we'll use the other one then," and if he says left you say, "Great, get rid of your right hand then." This is a crafty way to have them think the choice of hand is free, but you end up with the one with the ash hidden inside.

Now, light a cigarette, and let it burn down slightly so that you have some ash on the end. As far as your participant is concerned this is where the trick starts, so prepare to crank up the acting machine. Carefully tap the ash into your own palm, and put down the cigarette. Intone some mumbo jumbo – perhaps consider muttering about cosmic synchronicity, voodoo, or white witchcraft – any B.S. will do. Rub the ash into your palm and it will slowly disappear. Finally, all that remains is for you to ask him to open his hand, where he will find the ash has mysteriously appeared in his clenched fist. Sip that mocktail and bask in your glory.

SHOT-GLASS HUSTLE

Here's another game of Hanky-Poo. This one is a definite free-drink-getter — especially useful if you've spent your disposable income on this magic book. You place three shot glasses on the table, two facing mouth-up and one mouth-down. In three moves, flipping two glasses at a time, you'll end up with all three glasses facing mouth-down. What's more, you do it as quick as a flash and, guess what — no one else can replicate your magic, even if they copy your moves exactly. Their feeble attempts always result in at least one glass ending mouth-up. Fools.

HOW'S IT DONE?

This trick relies on two things. The first is your ability to make the moves quickly, thus confusing your sucker. The second is that when you set the glasses for his attempt, you subtly change the arrangement to one that makes it impossible to get all the glasses mouth-down in three moves. Never trust a magician.

Your demonstration begins with the two outer glasses mouth-up and the center one mouth-down [1]. The three moves are as follows and "right" and "left" is as you look at the glasses in front of you.

1

Move 1: Center and right-hand glass turned 180 degrees [2]

Move 2: Two outer glasses turned 180 degrees [3]

Move 3: Center and right-hand glass turned 180 degrees [4]

Yours will now all be mouth-down.

Now, set the glasses for your drinking partner, but, in a cunning reversal, place the two outer glasses mouth-*down* and the center glass mouth-*up* [5]. This subtle difference will not be spotted by the type of person who likes to combine betting and alcohol. If he follows your moves exactly he'll be bamboozled to find at least one of his glasses always ends mouth-up. Handy really, as it makes it easier to fill with the free drink you'll keep winning!

ARISE, SIR BENSON OF HEDGES

This trick is a moment of weirdness that you should quite easily be able to drop into your day-to-day life. In the process of opening your cigarette pack, one of the little suckers rises up and out on its own. You mention nothing of this blatant use of The Force and simply smoke it.

HOW'S IT DONE?

You'll need to prepare your cigarette pack in advance. I use a pack with a flip lid. Get yourself a paper clip and bend it into the shape shown here. This will be your secret lever that moves the cig. With a sharp knife, cut a slit in the back of the cigarette pack an inch in from the side, and which begins about a half-inch from the bottom and ends about the same distance from the hinge of the lid. If you are young or have dubious motor skills have someone help you with this.

Now, carefully insert the paper clip into the slit with the point upwards. Move it up and down to check it runs freely. While it's in the "up" position, push the tobacco end

of a ciggie on to the pointy bit of the paper clip and push down both the cig and the "lever" down into the pack.

To perform this telekinetic trick, set up the cig as described above, and put some more of the little tar sticks in the box to create the illusion that it's just a normal pack – don't wedge too many in though as you want to be able to move your prepared cig. You'll find that by holding the box with your left hand you can open the lid and move the paper clip on the back with your right hand. Try to make this unperceivable from the front. When the cig is almost all of the way out, put it to your lips and pull it off the paper clip. Close the lid and put your magic box away.

I never call attention to the fact I'm doing this trick, and I think that *not* performing it as a magic trick makes it so much more fun to do. If you try it in a public place you'll get some weird looks – mind you, if you're a magician, you're probably used to that.

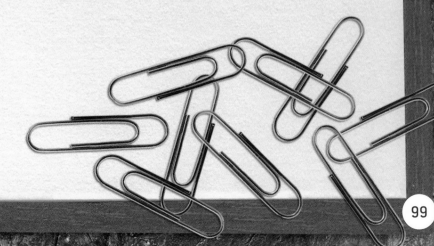

SLAMMER BAMMER

I have friends who can make drinks disappear – copious amounts. But imagine their surprise when I picked up a shot glass full of some barely legal substance, held it in my hands and made the whole shebang – drink *and* glass – vanish. Forget imagining – I'll tell you, they freaked out! Now you can do the same. I'm sharing this gem with you because I love you.

HOW'S IT DONE?

You are going to have to do a bit of craftwork to get this baby up and running. You need some strong elastic (about one-and-a-half feet in length), a safety pin and a bouncy ball. The bouncy ball should be big enough to wedge into the mouth of a shot glass, and, I'm afraid (but boy is it worth it) you need to thread the elastic right through the middle of it. Once you've managed this, tie a few knots at the end so the ball doesn't fall off. At the other end of the elastic attach a safety pin, to allow you to fasten the contraption to your jacket. The elastic should be long enough for you to reach but short enough to be sufficiently taut when held.

Now that you've created your gimmick, you need to pin it just below your jacket collar, and remember to wear your jacket [1]. Pick up your shot glass, containing your favorite poison, but make sure the glass isn't too full as it will need to accommodate the bouncy ball. You'll find it simple enough to reach back with your right hand and retrieve the ball – hold your hand naturally by your side and nobody will know the ball is there, especially as you'll be waving your

1

drink hand around as you get ready to down your shot. At this point, bring your right hand over your left and surreptitiously wedge the ball in the mouth of the glass. The glass should now be tethered securely to the elastic and the ball (in photo 2 my right hand has been removed for clarity). Hold the glass in an overhand fashion to conceal the ball from sight.

With both hands around the glass, keep your hands close to your body and lean forward a little, which will open your jacket ever so slightly [3]. At this point you should be looking at your hands, and they'll wonder what's going on. Now, however, you want to misdirect your audience for a moment, so look up and say, "Watch closely" or something like this, and everyone will look away from your hands and up to your face. On speaking, release the glass and allow the elastic to whip it back into your coat. Finally, focus all attention back on your hands where your audience will expect to see the glass, and dash their expectations by slowly pressing your hands flat together as if crushing it, and finishing with a final rub and an opening of your sweaty paws to show that it's disappeared.

TOP TIPS

When you are holding the elastic taut there will be some tension. Make sure that this doesn't show in your body language. Try to appear relaxed so your audience doesn't pick up on your sneaky stuff.

Definitely make sure you push the ball tightly into the mouth of the glass. If the glass falls on the floor it's terrible – you'll ruin the trick, and what a waste of decent booze!

CHAPTER 4

greasy spoon or haute cuisine, put them off their grub with some nauseating mealtime magic

ROLL WITH IT

Don't you just hate it when you get hard, stale bread in a restaurant? Nothing says business is slow more than stale restaurant bread. If you really want to make a point about the awful food, however, don't make a big song and dance about it – just grab one of the afore-mentioned rolls and bounce it like a basketball. Not only will you make onlookers laugh, but the management will probably put a special extra something in your tartar sauce. Yum yum!

HOW'S IT DONE?

This is a sight gag that never fails to get weird stares and double takes, but it takes a bit of practice. You need to be sitting at a table. Turn to your right and rest your left elbow on the table's edge. Hold the bread roll in your right hand at about head height, and prepare to *pretend* to throw the roll at the floor. Instead of actually flinging the savory product, however, quickly move your hand holding the roll downwards to below the edge of the table – moving your arm from the elbow.

Once your hand has passed out of sight and your arm is straight, tap your foot against the floor as if hitting the bass drum on a drum kit. For your audience, this will create the sound of the roll hitting the floor. Immediately, without moving your right arm upwards, turn your hand upwards and throw the roll into the air. This should be done through the wrist, not the arm – it's vital that the throw isn't seen by any spectators. All they should see is the roll flying up from beneath the table, at which point you skillfully catch it in your left hand.

Although quite lengthy in description this is a quickie to perform, but it's important that your timing is right and all the actions are smooth. And bear in mind that this trick is not restricted to just bouncing bread rolls; what about a coffee cup, a plate, a pair of earmuffs, or anything that is notoriously un-bouncy? I must admit, sometimes I do this trick using an actual bouncy ball. To anyone watching it looks like I'm just bouncing a ball, but *I* know there is so much more going on. Magicians are so self-indulgent!

SALT OR PEPPER?

Magic that happens in the spectator's hands is very strong. It makes the effect so much more special and memorable. This feat is a good example of that.

You're at a café, sandwich shop, or an establishment that sells baked potatoes. You grab a packet of salt from the counter and give it to someone to hold tightly in his hand. Suddenly, you pick up one of the pepper packets, rub the label, and it changes to salt, while your friend opens his hand to find that he's now holding the pepper packet in his kung-fu grip. You old master of spices, you!

HOW'S IT DONE?

To prepare this you'll need to obtain in advance the type of packets used by whatever seedy establishment you happen to be in. Packets clearly displaying "SALT" and "PEPPER" are the best, as it's easier for the spectator to follow what's happening. The gimmick in this trick is two packets – one salt, one pepper – stuck together, with each side showing a different condiment. With this in your pocket (and as long as the café isn't out of condiments) you're wired for sound!

Ahead of time, conceal a pepper packet in your right hand – no fuss, just hold it loosely in your fingers. Have the above-described double-facing pre-prepared packets in your left pocket. When you are ready to perform, grab a salt packet from the condiment dish and present it on your outstretched left hand [1]. Say that you want to show him something strange with the salt. While you are jabbering away, move your right hand (containing the concealed pepper packet) towards your left hand as if to pick up the salt packet there. In fact, *pretend* to pick up the salt packet –

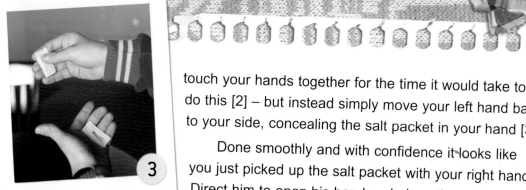

touch your hands together for the time it would take to do this [2] – but instead simply move your left hand back to your side, concealing the salt packet in your hand [3].

Done smoothly and with confidence it looks like you just picked up the salt packet with your right hand. Direct him to open his hand and place the pepper packet (still in your right hand) inside his, hiding any writing with your fingers [4], and have him close his hand tightly – clearly, he'll assume it's the salt packet he's holding.

While this is happening, dip your left hand into your pocket, leave the salt packet there and pick up the prepared double-sided packet. Now, keeping the gimmick concealed in your left hand, move it toward the packet bowl and pretend to pick one up. Demonstrate that you hold in your hand a pepper packet – clearly, it's important that the spectator only sees the pepper side of the gimmick. Hold it in your left hand in the way shown, and bring across your right hand as though to rub it in a mystical way – this will enable you to conceal the fact that you rotate the packet with your right thumb [5]. Incredibly, you now hold the salt [6]. This is a very magical moment for the audience, so allow it to sink in. Then, tell him to open up his hand slowly where, to his surprise, he finds *he* now holds the pepper! [7]

This one is a little tricky, so make sure you rehearse it well so that you are super-confident with the moves. If you put in the time and effort you'll have a doozy of a trick.

KNIFE SWALLOW

For years people have been amazed by the strange abilities of others, whether it be lying on a bed of nails, walking on hot coals, or swallowing swords. Let's face it, we all enjoy a good freak show. At your next social gathering, prove to your friends that you are part of this inbred family by swallowing a dinner knife. Quick, hide the silverware!

HOW'S IT DONE?

I love this one so much that I often do it on first dates. It's a great ice-breaker and chicks dig weirdos – at least, the ones in Chicago do. Position yourself at a table with your audience opposite, and place the knife on the table in front of you – it should be quite close to the edge, for reasons that will become clear in a moment.

Explain the ultra-dangerous feat you are about to perform and clear your throat in anticipation. The technique used to pick up the knife is crucial. Hold your hands in the manner demonstrated [1], and pick up the knife by sliding it off the edge of the table and into your hands [2]. Now, move the knife to your mouth, and tilt your head back in readiness. Keep your hands together – notice how the knife is concealed – and turn them ninety degrees to a vertical position as if you are about to

feed the knife down your throat [3]. Pause, relax, and pretend that something isn't quite right. Cough and hold your throat, and put the knife back on the table as you take a moment to "compose" yourself – you're not quite ready to perform such a potentially lethal trick just yet [4].

Repeat the action of picking the knife up, using the same technique, but instead of sliding the knife from the table's edge into your hands, let it fall into your lap [5]. This will go unnoticed by everyone as by this stage they aren't even looking for a funny move because they've seen you do this once already. You've conditioned them to buy your bullshit! I know – it's criminal, isn't it?

You must, of course, hold your hands in the same way as before, as though you are still holding the knife. Now, you're ready for the big finish – tilt your head back and apparently swallow the "knife," moving your hands downward as you pretend to push it down your throat. Make sure you demonstrate at the end that your hands are empty, take the admiration, and ask a waiter if you can have a whisk for dessert.

HAVE I GOT A ZIT?

This is another doozy from that Yankee Doodle Genius, Mac King. Mac has yet again managed to combine condiments and bodily fluids into a stomach-churning party piece.

You complain of a zit that is getting on your nerves, and you're concerned that it's really noticeable. You seek reassurance from a friend. Alas for him – however the poor onlooker responds, you proceed to squeeze that annoying pustule, squirting zit gravy all over him.

HOW'S IT DONE?

This one is easy-peasy, butter-squeezy! You need one of those butter packets found in cafés and cheap restaurants. Make sure it's been out of the fridge for a while so that it's really soft. Before presenting this wonder, pierce a hole in the foil wrapping with a pencil, about a quarter of a centimeter in diameter – I carry the butter packet in my pocket along with a tissue. When it's freak-out time, dip your hand into your pocket and grab the butter. Keep it concealed, and draw attention to an imaginary zit on your face – make sure everyone is looking at your head. Now bring the butter packet, still concealed in your hand, up to your face and, using both hands, give the butter inside a good squeeze – make sure the hole side of the butter is facing outward! Performed correctly, this should make the soft butter shoot out of the hole and through your fingers – preferably into the face of a nun. While the people freak out, move the now empty packet to your pocket, leave it in there, and grab the tissue. Use this to wipe any mess from your face and hands. It goes without saying that you *don't* offer the tissue to the nun – make her use her habit! Thanks, Mac.

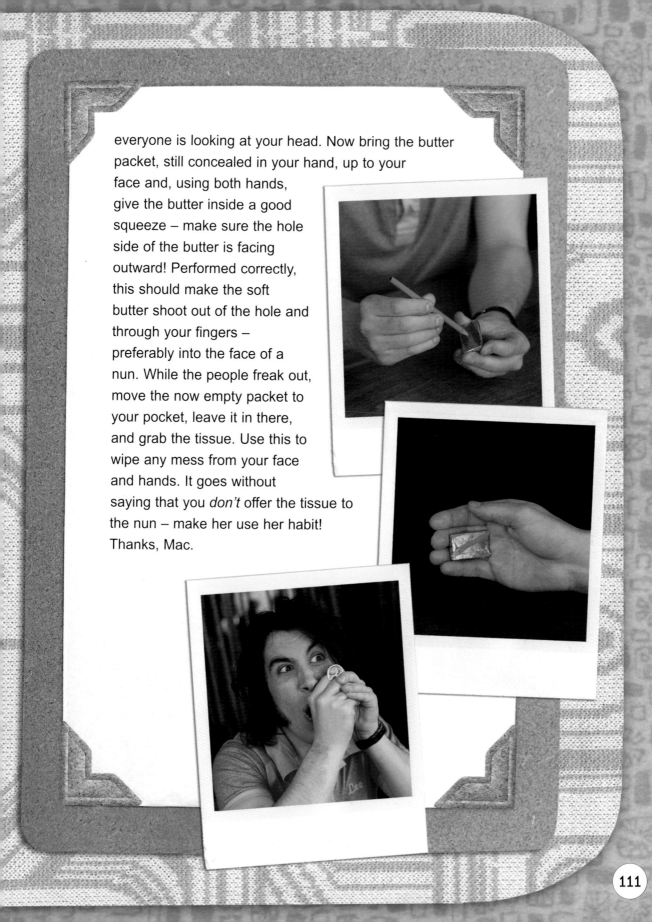

KARATE FIVER OF DEATH

This one is perfect if you're ever out walking in the woods, and want to break a stick with a five-dollar bill. I get the urge all the time! Honestly, though, this one's a miracle. You have an assistant hold a stick at both ends while you fold the note lengthwise. One sharp strike with this fiver's fold breaks the twig like . . . a twig? Of course, when your friends try to repeat the feat they struggle and look silly. Who said the dollar was weak?

HOW'S IT DONE?

This relies on blatant cheating! I love it! Get your assistant to grab the stick at each end, while you hold the note in the manner shown. Raise your hand and the note high, and prepare to bring it down quickly on the stick. However, as your hand comes down, flick out your right index finger behind the note, along its edge – your finger will break the stick. As soon as the stick has broken, pull your finger back in and no one, including the stick bearer, will be any the wiser.

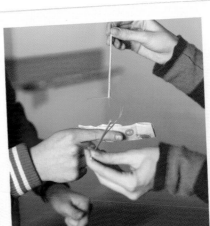

The "illusion" works because the vigorous action of swinging the note down disguises the smaller, quicker action of extending your index finger.

Of course, this trick need not be restricted to woodland play. For example, I have used it in restaurants with breadsticks. Use your imagination – be a little crazy!

I QUIT!

Having the ability to make cigarettes disappear is no big deal. My friend Andy goes through about sixty a day. Having said that, making a cigarette vanish in a smoke-free fashion is more impressive, especially if it's right under someone's nose. This trick delivers. You hold a borrowed ciggie in your sweaty little paw and in the blink of an eye it disappears faster than the ladies do at magic conventions.

HOW'S IT DONE?

The secret to this miracle lies in the devious use of a bodily fluid. No, before you get carried away, I'll tell you it's *saliva* – or "lick," as I call it. Before performing this one, get a good bit of lick on your right thumbnail. Pick up the cigarette with your left hand and put it into your right, and hold it the way the

lovely photograph demonstrates. While it looks as though you are holding it in your fist, your wet nail has been squeezed against the white tip of the cancer stick. Just a small amount of lick is all that's needed to stick it real good.

To make it vanish, all you have to do is open your right hand quickly, causing the cigarette to fall back against your thumb, still glued in place thanks to your sticky lick. Your audience won't see this at all because you'll be holding your palms in their face. To make the cigarette reappear quickly reverse the actions, swiftly bringing your thumb into your fist, and the cigarette will swing back over, giving the impression that you grabbed the cigarette out of thin air. This looks as good as the vanish. Hand him back his cigarette and feel proud that you just baffled him *and* put your lick on one of his cigs!

PSYCHIC STRAW

Any occasion on which you fool your friends into thinking you have telekinetic powers is awesome. This one allows you to do just that. You offer to substantiate your claim not by making someone hover, or something fly, but by moving a drinking straw on a table. Hey, come on, it's only a frickin' trick!

HOW'S IT DONE?

This one is really old, but I'm constantly surprised by the amazed reaction it gets from people – so it's in! You'll love it. You need a straight drinking straw, a bendy-wendy-crazy one won't do, and you also need to be sitting at a table. Place the straw on the table in front of you and hold your hand above it as if summoning every ounce of the mystical energy that makes straws move. This is all window-dressing and distraction, because while they're all looking at your hand . . . they don't see you blowing the straw! If you hold your mouth open a little you will be able to blow an undetectable stream of air toward the straw. The key to fooling everyone is to make no bodily movement as you blow, and to make no sound. With practice you will be moving straws all over your neighborhood, without, I hope, getting the reputation as the guy that blows.

KUNG-FU NANA

Being a sharing, generous person, you want to cut a banana into pieces. Trouble is, you're too damn lazy even to peel it. Before, something had to give, but not any more, because your amazing kung-fu strike takes care of this little problem.

Wanting chopped banana pronto, you strike the bent fruit twice. Lo and behold, when your friend or friendly grocer peels it, they find that you were true to your word — for it is cleanly divided into *three* segments; one for him and two for you. You need the potassium to keep that chop sharp!

HOW'S IT DONE?

Again, this one falls into my favorite-kind-of-magic category. All the preparation is done ahead of time, so you are free to put all your efforts into making the performance as convincing as possible.

You need a long needle. Carefully stick the needle into the banana, about a third of the way in from one end. Make sure that you push it as far as you can through the flesh, but not into or through the skin on the other side. Work the needle up and down, which will slice the nana inside its skin. Do the same at the other end of the banana and you are all set. I often prepare a banana while it's still part of a bunch, marking it in some way so I can tell it apart from the others. Pulling your pre-prepared banana from a bunch makes the trick look even less staged and more impressive.

When you are ready to rock, break off the banana you've prepared and begin your kung-fu moves. In classic, stereotypical martial-arts fashion, I favor two loud "HHHHIIIIIIYAAAA!!!!"s. All that remains is for you or one of your avid followers to peel the yellow peril, where they will discover that there is nana for everyone. You got the skills to pay the bills!

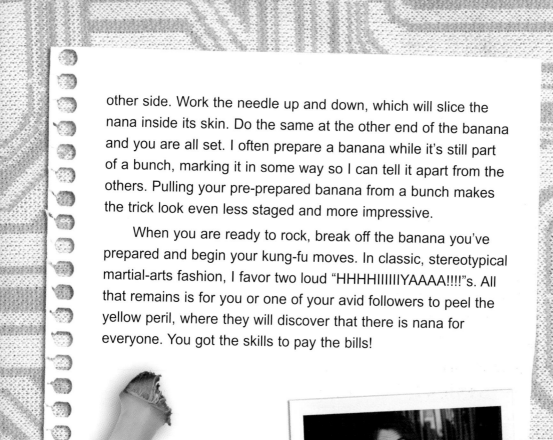

ON ME HEAD!

This one is an old sight gag that probably comes from the days of vaudeville – those variety acts popular in the early twentieth century. Done on the offbeat, though, it always gets a laugh.

Munching on some grapes, you draw your friends' attention to one of the little fellas that you are holding in your hand. You slap it on to the top of your head and it shoots out of your mouth – you wanna see a doctor for that!

HOW'S IT DONE?

Though ostensibly simple, this one requires some decent sleight of hand to make it believable. First, you need to have a grape hidden in your mouth. That's not hard – just chow down on a few, except for the last one you put in your mouth before you do the trick. That one must remain intact. Pluck another grape from the bunch and prepare yourself for the "false transfer!" This well-established trickery technique sounds daunting, but is actually simple. However, it does require some practice to make it look good.

Having pulled off another grape, hold it between the middle finger and thumb of your right hand. You are about to "pull focus" by the actions on the grape you are holding, as you can't say a great deal with the grape in your mouth! The idea, basically, is to pretend to take the grape from your right hand with your left hand. Once everyone has turned to you, hold your left hand open. Moving your right hand toward your left, turn your right wrist inward as you go, in essence concealing the grape from view – the intention is to mime, convincingly, that you are placing the grape in your left hand, and that the audience buy into this mime even if they can't see the grape itself. When the fruit is touching your left palm, keep hold of it in your right hand and begin to close the fingers on your left hand. When these fingers touch the back of your right hand move your right hand, still holding the grape, away to your right hand side and let your left hand close. The right fingers should hold the grape loosely so that the hand doesn't look like it's holding anything, while the left should appear to be holding a grape.

The above will take some time to master, so practice it all the time. Not just with grapes, though – use coins, anything. Just get it looking hot!

To finish this little wonder, slap your left hand (apparently containing the wee fruit) on your head and spit the concealed grape out of your mouth.

Like Derren frickin' Brown, I know what you are thinking! "Pete, what do I do with the grape in my right hand?" Easy, my friend. Lean over to the bunch of grapes and pretend to pull one off, but instead bring your concealed grape into view. Eat it and destroy all the evidence. You've earned that noble rot!

SOFT GLASS

This is a great trick to perform to friends after a wonderful meal. If you don't have any friends, you'll still get a kick out of doing it to yourself, although having to give yourself a round of applause is a little depressing.

You hungrily finish up your rum and coke and wrap the now empty glass in a napkin or newspaper and place it on the table. You tap the tabletop to prove that it's solid, and then, without prior warning, you slam the glass through the table and produce it from underneath. So impressed is the lady opposite you that she helps you scratch that itchy scab on your shin with her bare foot. What a gal!

HOW'S IT DONE?

This is one of the first tricks that I ever learned. You need to be seated at a table to perform it. Wrap your glass in some newspaper – newspaper is ideal as it has a certain stiffness that will be required in a moment – making sure that the edge of the newspaper runs along the mouth of the glass – effectively, keeping one end of the newspaper open.

Twist the paper at the opposite end so that the newspaper holds the shape of the glass.

Now, holding the glass-and-paper sculpture in your right hand, tap this against the table about a foot or so from the edge. In order to distract your admiring onlookers, you are now going to knock on the table in the same spot with your left hand – during which deception your secret move is going to happen. Move your left hand to the "knocking-spot" on the table, and at the same time move your right hand, holding the glass, back to the edge of the table. As you knock on the table with your left hand, while yammering all the while about how solid the table is, loosen your grip on the glass. You'll find that it will slide beautifully out of the paper and into your lap. Be careful that it doesn't roll off and smash on the floor. That happened to me once when I decided to perform this one after a couple of sherbets – bad idea.

You'll find that the paper will retain the shape of the glass if you handle it carefully. Move the empty husk of newspaper back to the spot on the table that you've fixated over throughout this trick, and smash your hand down on top of it. It crumples and you can screw it up and throw it away. Reach under the table as if to grab the glass, when in fact you're just picking it up from your lap.

A simple trick that always gets a great reaction.

BRAIN ANEURYSM

The magician in trouble is a standard plot in magic; this trick takes that to the extreme. During a normal day enjoying overpriced coffee at Starbucks, you complain of a headache. It persists to the point where you stand up and scream loudly, holding your head in pain as blood trickles from your temple. You collapse in a heap as everyone panics around you. You sit up again, take your coffee back to the counter, and scream: "I wanted decaf!"

HOW'S IT DONE?

I love this trick – it's one that freaks people out and probably oversteps the mark on bad taste, but who cares? To perform it, you'll need to wear a cap and make a little blood bag in advance.

Making a blood bag is easy. Go to a joke or theatrical supplies shop and buy some fake blood, the kind that will wash out of your clothes. Get some cellophane and cut a square 4 inch by 4 inch. Now, place it over the top of your left fist and poke it a little way inside between your fingers, effectively making a well. Carefully pour in some fake blood – from my experience a little goes a long way.

Twist the top of the cellophane and trim off any excess – you now have a blood bag! Simply place the bag just under the edge of your cap, close to your temple. Make sure the cap isn't too tight as the bag may burst prematurely.

That's it! All you have to do now is wait for the right moment. When with friends, fake not feeling too well, put your hands to your head as if in pain, and at the same time, squeeze the bag. Blood will come trickling down your face. String this out for as long as you can until you confess your prank. I like to wait until I'm on the stretcher in the ambulance as they usually give me a lift home!

MORE MAGIC . . .

Where do we go from here?

Well, my young scholars, we've walked a short way down the road. If you feel like you could get into this magic thing a little more seriously, below are some great resources I'm sure you'll find useful.

Genii – US magazine
www.geniimagazine.com

Magic – US magazine
www.magicmagazine.com

Magic Seen – UK magazine
www.magicseen.co.uk

Magic Week – UK-based Web site updated weekly with the latest news in the magic world.
www.magicweek.co.uk

There are loads of companies on the Internet selling magic tricks; below are a select few:

Hank Lee's Magic Factory – US magic shop
www.magicfact.com

Hocus Pocus – US magic shop
www.hocus-pocus.com

Alakazam Magic – UK magic shop
www.alakazam.co.uk

TV Magic – UK magic shop
www.tvmagic.co.uk

And for more about the author . . .

www.petefirman.co.uk

www.myspace.com/petefirman